HOMOEOPATHIC MEDI

A practical and handy guide for both
covering a wide range of ailments and their cures.

HOMOEOPATHIC MEDICINE FOR DOGS

A Handbook for Vets and Pet Owners

by

H.G. Wolff

Veterinary Surgeon

*Translated from the German
by A.R. Meuss* F.I.L., M.T.G.

THORSONS PUBLISHERS LIMITED
Wellingborough, Northamptonshire

First published in the United Kingdom 1984

First published in West Germany as *Unsere Hunde-gesund durch Homöopathie*
© Johannes Sonntag, Verlagsbuchhandlung, Regensburg, 1981

© THORSONS PUBLISHERS LIMITED 1984

British Library Cataloguing in Publication Data

Wolff, H.G.
    Homoeopathic medicine for dogs.
    1. Dogs—Diseases   2. Veterinary medicine
    Home, Homeopathic
    I. Title   II. Unsere Hunde-gesund durch
    Homeopathic. *English*
    636.7'0895532   SF991

    ISBN 0-7225-0809-3

**Printed and Bound in Great Britain by
Whitstable Litho Ltd., Whitstable, Kent**

Contents

Foreword

When it was first published in 1964, Dr H.G. Wolff's small *Gesunde Hunde* book (Fit and Healthy Dogs) soon became known and widely appreciated. This long awaited new edition has been greatly extended. With about thirty years' experience in small animals practice in a large city, practising the medicine taught by Hahnemann, and study visits to India, Japan and the USA, the author is probably better qualified than anyone else to tell us about the successes he has achieved in his field with homoeopathic remedies, and to invite us to 'imitate well', to quote Hahnemann.

Medical science has made enormous advances in recent years, with new chemotherapeutic agents constantly taking the place of older ones. Homoeopathy on the other hand has the great advantage that most homoeopathic remedies – *Arnica*, for instance, *Belladonna* and *Sulphur* – have been known for many centuries, have proved their value in popular medicine for generations, and have been tested in drug provings on healthy human subjects.

Physicians using the latest methods of treatment are forced to keep up with new developments all the time. A homoeopathic physician can concentrate on deepening his knowledge of the materia medica (pharmacology), learning more and more about the drugs he uses, and this gives him a firm foundation.

Homoeopaths do not prescribe on a particular diagnosis, but take full account of the physical and mental signs and symptoms the patient presents, practising individualized (personotropic) medicine.

Modern society, informed and achievement-orientated, is aware of the importance of preventive medicine, a field where natural remedies play a key role. There are now numerous societies which have made homoeopathy their cause and which have many members.

A book like this will no doubt meet with great interest from medical specialists, dog lovers and breeders alike.

DR HANS STOCK
Veterinary Surgeon

Preface to the Second Edition

The positive response to the first edition of this book in the many letters received, serves to indicate that there is great and general interest in homoeopathy; in particular in homoeopathy for animals.

Hearing and reading the reports on the successful treatment of dogs which had already been given up as beyond hope when their owners started to treat them using this book, both lay people and medical specialists must surely pause for thought.

Habent sua fata libelli – Books have their destinies. It is to be hoped that the second edition, too, will help to cure illness, relieve suffering, and indeed prevent trouble occurring.

Preface to the Third Edition

After just a year, a third edition of this book has become necessary - a sign that many are turning to natural methods of healing. The new edition has been enlarged and made more complete by the addition of medical information that has proved its value in practical experience.

Introduction

This book is dedicated to all animals, for they share this planet with man. All higher animals can produce symptoms and therefore be given homoeopathic treatment, just as human beings can. This particular volume is written specifically for dogs, however. The dog is the animal closest to man. Indeed, the philosopher Schopenhauer has called it 'man's greatest acquisition'.

Clearly there are many animal lovers all over the world who like to think for themselves and in the case of illness prefer a form of treatment that involves no synthetic chemicals, has no side effects and does not harm their pets. They are in favour of a method that ensures the health of the young even before they are born, by eugenic therapy given during pregnancy; and which when used in sickness has the effect of autovaccination, or immunization (vaccination as a method is not all that dissimilar), so that the animal gets fitter and more resistant with every disease it overcomes.

Homoeopathy is an active form of medicine. It reinforces the body's own healing powers and does not suppress them the way antibiotics and cortisone do. The individual is not deprived of his ability to help and heal himself, and nature's healing powers are not undermined. With homoeopathy, it is not the amount of chemical substance that matters, but the energies released by potentization of the medicinal agent. Homoeopathy gives a certain impetus, and if correctly applied this sets off natural regulatory processes in the organism that can overcome the disease. Its action is therefore rapid, safe and sure. Later generations will be able to appreciate this much more than we can, for the negative effects of current drugs legislation are bound to become fully obvious in due course.

Terms like 'autosuggestion' and 'placebo effect', commonly used to discredit homoeopathy in human medicine, have no place in the veterinary field.

Hahnemann's homoeopathy is a form of medical treatment that is not subject to changing fashions. Its basic principles have remained unchanged since they were first established early in the nineteenth century, though the method of application has changed.

Scientists are coming to realize more and more that gentle stimuli play a very important role in vital processes and in metabolism, and that tiny doses of certain substances such as hormones and vitamins can have very major effects. As a result, homoeopathy is also gaining increasing recognition.

Homoeopathy does not use powerful chemical agents to suppress troublesome symptoms. Instead, small doses of natural substances that given to healthy people produce the same symptoms as the disease does in a sick peson, are used to cancel and remove those symptoms. Homoeopathy supports the body's own efforts at healing and has no harmful side effects, a definite advantage over other methods of treatment and one that cannot be overestimated.

There are three basic principles underlying the whole of homoeopathy:

1. *Similia similibus curentur* – let likes be cured by likes. This holds true for all conditions where a specific stimulus will effect a return to normal function, i.e. a cure, making use of the body's own natural healing powers.

   It is known, for instance, that sulphur can both cause and cure skin eruptions, with the direction of action partly determined by the method of preparation. High doses will provoke skin changes, whilst small doses, in homoeopathic preparation, have the opposite effect, causing a reversal of action. Sulphur in homoeopathic doses will cure all skin eruptions similar to those provoked by sulphur in more substantial doses.

   What kind of skin eruption does sulphur cause?

2. Hahnemann said that, to answer this question, the drugs must be tested on healthy subjects. He and his successors have tested hundreds of drugs for their effects on healthy subjects. Their findings – known as the 'drug pictures' – are the key equipment of homoeopathic practitioners.

   Homoeopathic drug tests ('provings') done on animals differ very little from those done on humans. Animals are of course unable to give expression to the more subtle, subjective symptoms, but the characteristic objective guiding symptoms are of the same kind as in drug tests on humans. It is therefore perfectly all right to apply the findings of drug tests performed with humans to animals too.

In fact, more than 100 drug tests have already also been done with animals, most of them the painstaking work of the French veterinary surgeon Ch. Farré, carried out in his spare time. His findings confirm the above statement which has also been substantiated by others, among them M. Ferréol in Geneva, and the author.

Experience has also shown that – as Hahnemann himself has said – 'animals can be cured just as safely and surely by the homoeopathic method as human beings can'.

3. The third principle is that of using very small doses of the potentized medicine. Their action lies below the threshold of material doses and represents one of the greatest triumphs of homoeopathy, for it means that, when correctly used they cannot produce any toxic effects. Even the smallest whelp can be treated in complete safety. Homoeopathic medicines are not merely diluted but also potentized, i.e. thoroughly shaken (succussed) or ground up (triturated) with the diluting agent, and through this method of preparation homoeopathic drugs gain enormously in medicinal power.

The higher the potency (i.e. the greater the number of stages of dilution and potentization), the greater is the specific medicinal power – providing its drug picture closely matches the symptoms of the recipient. Potencies of 1:100 are available, and 1:1000, and even figures with 30, 200 and 1000 zeros. At those levels the action no longer comes from material forces, but from immaterial radiations in the form of waves that have a direct effect on the vitality of the organism, on that ordering principle which maintains life, departing from the body at death and leaving it to break down into its chemical constituents.

One might also say that one is dealing here with subatomic energies, with emanations that have curative powers providing that the remedy has the right wave-length, i.e. is similar to the image presented by the disease in the form of symptoms.

This is where a television journalist, reporting on homoeopathy as an 'expert', revealed his ignorance. Derisively, he drank down a dose of a high potency at the end of the programme, calling it impure alcohol, his aim being to prove that it had no effect. But that is the point of it: the question is one of mind over matter, i.e. thought has to determine the issue, in this case the drug diagnosis. This is the key that unlocks the treasure house of this school of medicine, treasures that of course are not immediately accessible to everybody.

Homoeopathy involves energy acting on the smallest of particles. Even Lao-tze, the great Chinese philosopher, was aware of the fact that the weak can overcome the strong; softness the hardest material. 'Everybody knows this', he complained, 'but none will act on it.'

Homoeopathy makes use of these principles. Using the indicated remedy as a medicinal stimulus, we set in motion the body's own regulatory processes, to overcome the disease. With continued 'surges of response' the body learns the 'technique of victory' (an expression coined by K.V. Roques), overcoming the enemy disease. The principle is the same as with any form of immunization. The specific medicinal stimulus induces the body to effect its own cure, emerging from the disease state fitter and more resistant than before, for as already stated, every homoeopathic treatment is a form of micro-vaccination.

x (1:10), c (1:100) and also LM (1:50,000) potencies are recommended in this book. It is not possible to accept the reality of this type of active principle if one uses the ordinary concepts that are limited to the sphere of matter. But it does nevertheless exist. The most striking cures are in veterinary medicine, too, achieved particularly with LM potencies.

The border between the last potency still containing molecules of the original substance and one containing no such molecules lies between $23x$ and $24x$, between $9c$ and $10c$, and between $3LM$ and $4LM$. The medicinal actions of potencies beyond that border are due to a dynamic factor, not to any molecules of substance.

This is the reason why the experimental pharmacological studies used in orthodox medicine are pointless when it comes to demonstrating homoeopathic drug actions and must be rejected as such. Homoeopathic drugs can only be tested in drug provings on healthy subjects, or on patients. No science, thinking only in materialistic terms, is therefore able to make an authoritative statement on homoeopathic remedies. It is incomprehensible that laws relating to that approach sould be forced upon those who are basing their work and thoughts on completely different premises. It should be noted that from the homoeopathic point of view, the issue of costly laboratory studies loses its significance, for the simple reason that homoeopathy is not confined to physical parameters.

The science-based medicine taught in our medical schools claims to be the only authoritative method of treatment. There are however a great many methods outside the 'orthodox' which are based on observation, and which are highly efficient. The modern practitioner can choose which method is the best in any given case, provided of course he knows a number of these many different methods of treatment. Not every illness, for instance, may be curable with homoeopathy. Dietary errors are best corrected by diet, a foreign body needs to be removed manually or surgically, and with certain infections, antibiotics will be required to destroy the bacteria that cause them. When limits have been reached that no other means will help to undo, surgery may have to be resorted to. When an organ has become atrophic, homoeopathy cannot be expected to achieve regeneration, being a method employing a specific medicinal stimulus on tissue that is still able to react and thus initiate the healing process.

There still remain a very large number of conditions that will respond to homoeopathic treatment, and many of the most important of these are discussed in this book.

In a lecture given at Leipzig, Hahnemann said:

The closer the correspondence between the morbid symptoms of the remedy chosen and the symptoms of the sick animal, the more definitely and also the more rapidly and lastingly will the illness of that animal be cured, with a certainty that comes very close to a mathematical certainty.

Surely only an inexperienced and dull-witted observer would ever want to deny that animals show symptoms of their disease just as well and as clearly as men do. They have no speech, but the many changes that can be noted in their appearance, their behaviour and their natural and vital functions serve as a perfect substitute for speech.

An animal knows nothing of pretence, nor does it – like man – exaggerate its expression of pain, or hide its feelings and invent symptoms that do not exist. Man is so often swayed one way or the other in this, being ruined by his upbringing, rotten in his morals, or driven by his passions. It is immediately obvious that everything the animal reveals of its disease through symptoms is indeed a true expression of its inner state, and the pure, true image of the disease.

In a word, animals can be cured just as safely and surely by the homoeopathic method as human beings can.

Perhaps I may have the honour on another occasion to speak to this distinguished assembly on the equipment and treatment of stables for sick animals.

This much for today, then, with the signal set at least for an effective way to rid our domestic animals, that mean so much to us, of their diseases.

For these poor creatures, unable to call their tormentors to account, also deserve the compassion of every humane citizen.

Homoeopathic treatment is of course less easy with animals than it is with humans, who after all are able to express themselves in words. We have to depend on the objective symptoms only. If there are not enough symptoms or other circumstances to lead to the choice of a single remedy, one will have to use two or three in combination, as a matter of necessity. This does of course fall short of the ideal of the homoeopathic practitioner, which is to cover the whole morbid situation with a single remedy. Sometimes it is simply unavoidable.

Homoeopathic drugs can be given when the first signs of an illness appear, e.g. *Aconitum* when the onset is febrile, even if the final diagnosis is not yet certain and medical aid not immediately available. In fact it is often possible to prevent a disease from developing by giving the indicated drug in good time. The name of a disease is on the whole irrelevant, although the usual scheme has been followed in this book, to make orientation easier.

This book is primarily designed for veterinary surgeons who are aware that homoeopathy offers a wide range of possibilities for closing many of the gaps that currently exist in their conventional curative arsenal but who would like some practical guidance.

Technical terms have been deliberately limited to assist the many animal lovers who are interested in the subject. For those who like to think for themselves, this book intends to provide certain suggestions as to how they can take preventive action in health and effect a cure in case of sickness. In the present age, when we are more deeply than ever caught up in material things, the publication of a book such as this may prove of great benefit.

Health is a great treasure, and to maintain it in the face of all the risks that life presents is a major achievement. This holds true for all living creatures. Schopenhauer said in his *Aphorismen zur Lebensweisheit*: 'Taking it altogether, nine tenths of our fortunes depend entirely on our state of health. If you have it, everything becomes a source of enjoyment — it is by far the most important thing for human happiness. Beauty is in part related to health.'

Loving concern for all creatures is nowhere more completely expressed than in the Buddhist *Metta Sutta*. In that book, health and freedom from pain are part of the peace and happiness desired for all creatures, both men and animals:

> May all creatures be happy
> and find peace.
> All living creatures that exist,
> be they strong or weak,
> large or small,
> visible or invisible
> far or near,
> born or as yet unborn –
> may there be happiness for all of them.

Homoeopathic Drugs

1. Decimal potencies are indicated by the letter x, centesimal potencies by the number only or sometimes by the letter c.

2. Acute conditions require a frequent curative stimulus, with a dose given every quarter-hour, half-hour, hour or two hours. In chronic conditions, medication is given less frequently. It should be noted however that the duration of action given for high potencies in human medicine is usally less in animals (only half as long as a rule), with biological processes running their course more quickly in different animal species.

3. The potency is of secondary importance in the treatment of acute conditions, as any potency will be helpful. The opposite holds true for chronic conditions, for these always require the stimulus of a relatively high potency. The potencies stated are approximate indications as experienced homoeopaths will vary them depending on the state of the disease.

4. When a dog develops a febrile condition with temperatures above 39°C/102°F, a few doses of *Aconite 6x* or *30* will take the sting out of the disease. After this – or in cases where the condition is only noted at a later stage – *Belladonna 6x* or *30* is given hourly until the symptoms abate. If instead the symptoms become more marked, i.e. the condition has not yielded to those first doses, a remedy is selected according to the indications given in the different sections.

5. It should always be remembered that this medication represents curative stimuli. It is not a matter of quantity or weight. In this respect homoeopathic medicines differ from all other pharma-

ceutical products. A hundred tablets taken at one go have no greater effect than a single tablet or half a tablet that is crushed and placed on the tongue.

Whether it is a Yorkshire Terrier or a Great Dane, therefore, the dose will always be the same: 1 tablet, or 5–10 drops, or half a teaspoon of the powder. The most important factor is that the stimulus is given at specific intervals.

Something we cannot stress highly enough is the fact that given in the right way, these drugs cannot have toxic effects.

The well-known joke by Zille is certainly true:
A women arrives at the doctor's surgery very excited, with her young daughter, and tells him that the child has eaten all the homoeopathic medicine at one go.
'With or without the package?' the doctor asks.
'Without' is the answer.
'That's all right then,' says the doctor.
The reason why should now be clear.

6. Another important advantage speaks for itself: chemical products cost more than homoeopathic drugs do.

Administration of Drugs

The administration of drugs presents no problem. Homoeopathic remedies have many advantages and no disadvantages. They are practically tasteless and without smell and are largely absorbed via the papillae of the tongue.

If a tablet is to be given, it is broken down into powder on a small piece of paper, then the jaws are opened and the powder poured onto the moist tongue. It will adhere and the dog will be aware of having been given something that tastes good. Intelligent animals will later take the medicines of their own accord, probably also because they realize that they do them good. Once a cure has been effected most animals will refuse medication, despite the fact that it still has the sweet taste of lactose. Another way is to put the medicine in water or milk, or a mixture of the two. It is also a good method to pick up the powdered tablet with a moistened finger and apply it directly to the gums or tongue.

Fluid medicines (dilutions) taste slightly of alcohol. 5-10 drops of the medicine are added to a spoonful of milk or water and poured between the lips without opening the jaws. This will prevent choking. Another useful method is to use a small dog biscuit or rusk as the vehicle, providing all of it is eaten.

Homoeopathic medicines are occasionally also presented in powder form (trituration). In that case, the ideal dose is just under half a teaspoon.

As to duration of treatment, the indicated remedy is given until symptoms disappear, decreasing the dose as the condition improves. Homoeopathic medicines are never continued 'to be on the safe side'.

Dosage unless otherwise stated, is: for acute conditions, 1 tablet or 5-10 drops every half-hour or one- to two-hourly, depending on progress; for chronic conditions, a dose is given once or twice daily.

From a Letter to an Animal Lover

I am happy to answer your queries.

Homoeopathic preparation means that the original substance which may have little or no effect on the organism in its natural state (e.g. gold, platinum, calcium, silicon, lycopodium) is processed to develop its medicinal properties.

This processing does not consist of 'dilution'. The special method used in homoeopathic pharmacy — increasing the potency step by step, always with vigorous shaking — results in a decrease in the amount of substance present, but an increase in the energies of the drug. A 30th or 200th potency no longer contains a single molecule of the original substance, but the biological energy has increased enormously. Given drop by drop, it will, however, develop its medicinal action only in a patient whose biological structure shows potential, i.e. energetic agreement with it, as is also evident from the similarity between the symptoms of the disease and the symptoms of the drug. Anyone who has not actually seen the experiment will find it hard to believe, but it is true nevertheless.

Some of the best cases in my practice are the cures achieved with high potencies, using the *30x* or *30c,* a *200, 1M* (1,000) or even *10M.* A certain type of viciousness in dogs for example can be cured only with a single dose of *Hyoscyamus 10M.*

As to how and why — if you weigh a substance that may be made into a medicament, you merely establish a single fact, that it relates in a certain way to gravity. There are, however, numerous other qualities that cannot be weighed. These are the intramolecular and interatomic energies. We know from modern physics that they are beyond our range of comprehension.

The homoeopathic method of preparation causes changes in the solvent that relate to those nuclear energies. The medicinal substance which until then was in the form of matter is changed into biological energy. In homoeopathy, the process is known as potentization. A potency produced by this method will correct a disturbed biological equilibrium, so that the vital energy can function normally again. The result is that the patient recovers.

It is necessary of course — and this is where the art comes in — that the drug must match the disorder. It has to have the same wave-length, just as a wireless is tuned to a certain station, otherwise it will have no effect, missing the mark. This also explains why the wrong remedy will have no harmful effects and the reason why certain symptoms one observes must always be present, as a base line, to enable us to differentiate a particular remedy among the many that are available. Homoeopathy is not based on explanations, as is the medicine taught in most medical schools, but on observation.

Experience has shown that low dilutions have an effect 'only' on the physical body, higher ones on our vital energy, higher ones still on our moods and feelings (for homesickness, a dose of *Ignatia 30*), and that with the highest potencies we finally also reach the mental functions (viciousness). The higher functions in turn affect the lower ones. This is why very high potencies can also be very useful in dealing with physical problems, if these are due to lack of equilibrium in the higher functions.

Practical experience has shown that in man and also in the higher animals it is the higher functions that are more important (the vital force, or that which holds the body together — every religion has a term for it), because they create the body and maintain it. The body is merely the product of those higher potentials, and normal function depends on their equilibrium.

Scientific proof will probably only be forthcoming when atomic research is further advanced. At present, potencies are a matter of empirical medicine (medicine based on observation). There is no explanation as yet, but millions of observations have been made.

In conclusion it may be said that all homoeopathic drugs act at the energic level, even if there is still 'something in it' and they have not yet become 'intangible'.

In this materialistic age, orthodox medicine may also be referred to as 'scientific materialism', with validity given only to things that are weighable, measurable, and reproducible in time and space. Fortunately there are also other views on life, and the key question in the minds of all thinking people is this: Is the creative principle in the universe substantial and perceptible to the senses, or is it rather spiritual by nature, a form of energy, and therefore not perceptible to our sense organs?

All religions hold the latter point of view. The physicians of antiquity also knew this. The word 'medicament' derives from the Latin *medica mente* which literally means to heal through the spirit. That is the true nature of medicine ...

Extract from a letter written on 24 January 1965

1. Diseases Affecting the Head

Eyes

Stye or Hordeolum

Dogs, like humans, occasionally develop a stye, a small swelling on the edge of the lid that can be very troublesome to the patient. Ointments are a nuisance, but *Staphisagria 6x*, given several times a day, will achieve a rapid cure. If the condition is very painful, *Hepar sulphuris 3x*, the classical remedy for suppuration, will be useful if given every two hours.

Tear Duct (Lacrimal Canal)

Continuous lacrimation (flow of tears) on one or both sides, with no visible change in the outer eye, is due to inflammation causing a blockage in the nasolacrimal duct. If irrigation of the duct with something to reduce the inflammation does not give the desired result, *Staphisagria 6x* may be used, and also *Silicea 12x* until the condition has cleared.

Warts (Papillomas)

Surgery should not be one's first choice if papillomas develop on the lids. It does not treat the cause. Treatment with homoeopathic remedies consists in first of all giving the remedy that will correct the disturbed metabolic equilibrium which has led to wart formation. The warts will then regress. Fifty per cent of warts will be found to disappear when *Thuja 6x* is given three times daily. If there has been no change for the better after two weeks, *Causticum 12x* is used next, if necessary followed with *Acidum nitricum 6x*, always for the same length of time.

Here one sees one of the great and inestimable advantages of homoeopathy: if the remedy has not been correctly chosen and therefore does not fit, it does not harm the organism. It 'misses the mark', leaving no side effects. It needs exactly the right medicinal stimulus to trigger the body's own tremendous power to heal itself — which in this case has been blocked. It will restore the former state of health wherever possible. Failures are due to the choice of the wrong remedy, not to lack of effectiveness.

If the papillomas show no change after all this and it becomes necessary to remove them surgically, experience has shown that there is normally no recurrence.

Graphites 12x may be the remedy to treat dermoid and sebaceous cysts if the dog is heavy, running to fat, and always shows a good appetite.

Conjunctiva

Acute conjunctivitis is generally due to a chill, a draught, and to the dust and dirt from car exhausts. When only one side is affected, the owner quite often admits that the window was open when driving and the dog was sitting in the resulting draught. The inflamed conjunctiva is red and swollen, and there is a copious discharge of hot, excoriating fluid. These symptoms are found in the drug picture of *Euphrasia* (eyebright) which is given internally, in the *3x* potency, every one or two hours. In addition the eye may be bathed with a *Euphrasia* solution, using 10 drops of the tincture in ½ glass of warm isotonic saline (1 tablespoon of salt to a litre of water).

Apis 3x is very effective against allergic oedema of the conjunctiva.

In chronic conjunctivitis one often sees a thick, greeny yellow discharge, as in distemper. *Pulsatilla 4x* is the remedy for this.

Sometimes, when the condition has not been properly treated, or not treated at all, the inflammation may have spread to the eyeball, which then appears blood-shot, with the vessels standing out clearly. *Belladonna 4x-6x* will be useful in these cases. There is no need to mention that the condition is extremely painful and accompanied by marked photophobia (sensitivity to light) — something to be taken into account when giving treatment. This is a clinical picture that was commonly seen on the Continent when distemper was widespread after the Second World War. It always occurred just before convulsions developed. *Belladonna 6x,* alternating with *Apis 3x* at hourly intervals, gave good results.

Chronic lacrimation (flow of tears) resisting all treatment may also be due to a constitutional disorder. It then acts as a valve for a metabolic disorder. This is usually an imbalance in salt (sodium chloride) metabolism, and the remedy is *Natrum muriaticum 12x*, three doses a day for ten days.

A change of diet is vital in these cases. No more food mixes or tinned foods — fresh foods should be given instead (see *Natrum muriaticum* Type, Chapter 17).

Terriers are prone to a particular type of inflammation - blepharitis (inflammation of hair follicles of the margin of the lids). The follicles are swollen and projecting in the conjunctiva and on the inside of the nictitating (involuntarily blinking) membrane, and constant friction against the cornea causes chronic irritation and even ulceration.

If *Argentum nitricum 6x* does not effect a cure in eight to ten days, surgical treatment should be considered.

Excessive discharge of tears, but no redness, due to draughts or wind	*Pulsatilla 6x* *Euphrasia 3x* in equal parts 3-4 times daily
Reduced flow of tears 'Dry Eye' combined with local application of physiological saline, eye ointments and vitamins A and E	*Kalium bichromicum 12x* if nose and mucous membranes are dry
	Lycopodium 30x once a day if combined with disorders of the liver, appetite and digestion

Changes in the Cornea

The cornea can be injured when playing with other dogs or with cats, by foreign bodies (chaff and hay seeds), or if it is hit by branches when rushing through the undergrowth. Soon, whitish material (a 'film') will form near the surface of the cornea which becomes opaque and grey and looks dull.

The first remedy to be used is *Mercurius sublimatus corrosivus 6x*, four times daily, with *Euphrasia* ointment or *Euphrasia* lotion applied locally to reduce inflammation.

The same applies for keratitis (corneal opacity) caused by distemper or metabolic disease. In this case the changes are not so close to the surface, which remains smooth, but deeper down. Clearing the condition will of course take longer in these cases, and treatment sometimes has to be continued for weeks.

A superficial inflammation can easily develop into a corneal ulcer with a sharply defined crater, the base of which is covered with purulent material. *Kalium bichromicum 6x* is the remedy for this condition, if the crater looks as if punched out.

If a system of red blood vessels appears on the cornea in the course of treatment, easily visible to the naked eye, *Aurum 6x* is the remedy to give at this stage.

If marks and scars remain once the condition has been cured, *Conium 6x* three times a day should be given as a follow-up treatment, followed by *Calcarea carbonica 12x* if indicated.

When corneal ulcers do not have sharp margins, *Mercurius sublimatus corrosivus 6x* is given several times daily.

Apis 3x follows on if there is marked swelling of the conjunctiva, *Calcarea carbonica 6x* to make up defects in the epithelium.

Cataract, Amaurosis and Glaucoma

These three conditions only respond to treatment to a limited extent. Early diagnosis and treatment coupled with perseverance — for it is long-term treatment which is required — will however give results in many cases, leading to arrest or even improvement.

Cataract is a familiar condition, with opacity developing in the lens. In the end, the lens appears more or less white or grey, so that vision is as though through opaline glass. Sight is correspondingly impaired, and natural compensation occurs in that orientation is increasingly based on the sense of smell.

Practically every dog develops senile cataract at around the age of ten, with the early signs of this apparent some time in advance. This type of cataract can be inhibited with

> *Calcarea fluorica 6x*
> *Natrum muriaticum 12x*
> *Magnesia carbonica 6x*

Three doses of one remedy daily in rotation, continuing four weeks.

Amaurosis, or black cataract, unfortunately cannot be treated. It is due to poisoning with endogenous or external toxins, or inflammatory disease of the brain, retina or visual nerve. The pupillary reflex is absent, i.e. the pupil does not contract to light but remains wide open and immobile.

Again the sense of smell will assist orientation, and many owners only become aware of the problem when the furniture in their home has been moved to different places. The dog will then run into it, thus indicating that it has for quite some time been suffering from an eye condition that is not painful but also does not respond to treatment.

The situation is somewhat better in a case of glaucoma. Here the internal pressure in the eye is increased, and the excess pressure causes swelling of the eye. This in turn results in damage to the visual nerve and the retina. The greater and more prolonged the pressure, the more severe is the resulting damage, finally leading to blindness. The disease may occur on its own, or in conjunction with other eye conditions.

Increased intraocular pressure will make the dog irritable. Photophobia and lacrimation (discharge of tears) are also noted. To start with, *Belladonna 6x* is given several times daily to combat the local inflammation, together with a single dose of *Phosphorus 30x* daily at night. The eye is bathed with *Euphrasia* eye lotion (10 drops of the mother tincture to half a glass of lukewarm isotonic saline) when required, and *Euphrasia 4x* is also given internally, until the condition improves.

Unfortunately, glaucoma is often only diagnosed when it has fully developed. *Phosphorous 200*, given mornings and evenings for one week, will stop the condition from developing further and usually results in steady improvement.

A greenish pupillary reflex is frequently noted with glaucoma, which is also why it has sometimes been called 'green cataract'.

Surgical treatment for cataract is not advisable, as the situation is not the same as for humans. The only result would be differences perceptible in light intensity. Removal of the lens makes the eye extremely long-sighted. Dogs cannot be provided with spectacles to correct this, the way humans can.

There are said to be ways of improving lens opacity by giving vitamins and liver remedies, but the results so far have not been convincing.

Ears

Inflammation of the Outer Auditory Canal, Otitis externa, Canker

A dog with inflammation of the outer ear — a very common condition among our four-legged friends — will scratch the ear, shake his head and not infrequently sweep along the floor with the affected part, or he may try and rub the ear against the leg of a table.

If the otitis is one-sided, he will hold the head at an angle, and the continuous irritation will make him extremely restless. The condition is painful even in mild cases, where the only sign is a copious discharge of brown fluid. In severe cases, the dog presents a picture of utter misery, and there is an evil-smelling discharge which may be fluid or purulent.

If the symptoms are minor, the ear is cleaned daily with cotton wool, until the cotton wool at the end of a wooden stick or swab comes out clean. *Calendula* ointment on a fresh piece of cotton wool is then applied (or *Calendula* tincture instilled drop by drop).

After this, the external auditory canal is gently massaged by hand from the outside. If the reddening of the canal is not too marked, a few doses of *Belladonna 6x*, given internally at two-hourly intervals will cure the condition.

Caught early, canker is not a serious problem. Treatment of a badly inflamed ear on the other hand involves considerable effort. Great care and patience are required. Catarrh of one or both ears may often be the outward sign of severe metabolic disorders, with the auditory canal used as a valve to discharge toxins, for instance if the liver and kidneys, the actual organs designed for detoxification, are no longer able to cope. If the inflammation is limited to the right side the possibility of liver and intestinal disorders should be taken into account; if it is leftsided, ovarian malfunction may be the cause.

In a case of external otitis limited to the right ear, therefore, feeding errors should be enquired into. In most cases, a more or less chronic intestinal disorder is present, due to the diet containing too high a proportion of tinned and other convenience foods. Changing to a raw food diet will often already be half the cure.

External otitis limited to the left ear may be connected with a hormonal imbalance. It may sometimes be due to hormone injections given for suppression of oestrus (heat). In this case, local treatment needs to be combined with specific treatment of the organic condition (see Regulation of Hormonal Imbalance, page 91).

Calendula tincture is a certain cure for inflammations of the external canal.

The undiluted tincture is put into the external ear once daily, using a drop bottle or disposable syringe, and the ear is then lightly massaged. At the same time, 5-10 drops of *Calendula 3x* are given internally two or three times daily. This will get the condition under control relatively soon, and the animal is saved from a painful illness and also the danger of relapse if efforts are at the same time made to identify the possible causes of the inflammation (food, allergies, digestive disorders).

If the dog has already had cortisone therapy, the damage caused by this will of course make the process, normally a short one, somewhat longer.

Bilateral discharge of foetid pus, yellow and sometimes with traces of blood, aggravation at night and worse for warmth, calls for *Mercurius sublimatus corrosivus 6x* four times daily.

If the ear is particularly painful, and basically any ear infection is painful, so that the dog is intolerant of the least touch, barking and biting as one tries to examine it, veterinary surgeons usually consider anaesthetizing it, so that the ear can be effectively treated. A homoeopath on the other hand knows that this calls for *Hepar sulphuris 6x*. The inflammation is reduced after a few doses and with this also the pain and the nervousness. This applies particularly in cases where the pus smells of old cheese and contains blood.

If the wax has the appearance and consistency of honey and is produced in copious amounts — and perhaps there is also some eczema around the muzzle and eyes — and if in addition the patient is very obese, chilly and constipated (thyroid hormone deficiency), *Graphites 4x* is the remedy.

Petroleum 8x is useful when there is plenty of wax but the skin is relatively dry and thickened and there are fissures or weeping eruptions. Petroleum otitis has the characteristic feature of getting worse in winter. Travel — by car, train or boat — is also a problem, as the dog tends to vomit.

Silicea 12x, three times daily for some time, will be considered if discharge from the ear has persisted for some time and therefore become chronic. The *Silicea* discharge is foul-smelling, thin and excoriating. *Silicea* patients are always somehow weakly and notably sensitive to cold.

Psorinum 30x is useful if the discharge is a yellowy brown, is very irritating and smells very strongly of boiled meat. The discharge may have persisted for some time, sometimes at intervals over many years. The most important symptoms are marked chilliness, voracious appetite, and eruptions with that special smell. Symptoms occur in winter and disappear in the summer.

Warts in the ear are treated with *Calcarea carbonica 30x* in the mornings and *Causticum 12x* at night, 1 tablet, until they are definitely regressing or disappear.

Foreign bodies (awns of wild barley, chaff) may be the cause if there is a sudden, one-sided inflammation of the external auditory canal.

It has already become obvious that the smell of an infected ear can be a useful pointer in the choice of the remedy:

If the discharge smells strongly of cheese, *Hepar sulphuris 6x* will be required (possibly followed with *Silicea 6x).*

If the discharge smells of boiled meat, *Psorinum 30x* will help, and a smell of herring brine is an indication for *Acidum nitricum 6x.*

Excoriating discharges call for *Sulphur 6x.*

Acute redness of the inner ear requires *Belladonna 6x*, chronic redness *Sulphur 6x*. Eczema on the inside of the external ear is an indication for *Sulphur 12x* and *Graphites 12x*, four times daily in alternation.

Swellings in the canal or outer ear are treated with *Graphites 4x*, with Cocker Spaniels receiving *Argentum nitricum* in addition.

If ear inflammations are treated not only locally but also internally, using the appropriate remedy, surgical treatment will hardly ever be necessary, and the cure will always be a genuine one.

Haematomata (blood blisters) in the ear flaps are treated with the following mixture:

> *Arnica 6x*
> *Hamamelis 3x*
> *Bellis perennis 2x*

in equal parts, 10 drops every two hours, until there is an improvement. At the same time the ear is massaged two or three times a day with *Arnica* ointment, until the effusion disappears, though in the case of older dogs this may take weeks.

Otitis media (Inflammation of the Middle Ear)

If all the symptoms described in the previous section are present but there are none of the local signs such as redness, discharge or swelling, otitis media is the likely diagnosis.

Pulsatilla 200, one dose morning and night for two days only (or *Pulsatilla 6LM*, 5 drops three times daily for one week) will help.

Eczema in the Margin of the Ear, Sarcoptic Mange

Eczema in the margin of the ear, usually a chronic condition and particularly common in Dachshunds, presents as whitish, scaly lesions, with slight bleeding from the area. It is treated with *Silicea 12x*. It is advisable to massage an antifungal ointment into the ears at the same time, as fungus infection is common in these cases. *Silicea 12x* needs to be given three times daily for a considerable period. If there is a risk that persistent head shaking will cause the crusts which have formed to break open again, the loose ears are folded back over the head and held in position with a net or a head bandage. It is of course important to ascertain that the head shaking is not due to inflammation of the auditory canal. When *Silicea* has ceased to bring progress after some time, *Acidum fluoricum 6x* is used to follow on.

Sarcoptic mange may be another cause of head shaking. This is an inflammation of the auditory canal caused by mites.

Where the usual antiparasitic preparations, the most effective form of treatment, are not tolerated, *Calendula* ointment has proved helpful.

The canal is cleaned once a day and the ointment applied, for a period of at least five days.

Leather Ear, Contraction of Scars on Cropped Ears, Keloids

Silicea 12x is also the remedy of choice for the condition known as leather ear, where the tips of the ears grow hairless to begin with, and later the whole ear is involved. Long-term treatment is necessary, following the *Silicea* with *Calcarea fluorica 12x* if indicated.

Externally, the ear should be massaged with baby oil.

Contracted scars on the ear and keloids require *Graphites* and *Silicea*, both in the *12x*, given four times a day on alternate days. Contraction of the scars has a bad effect on the position of the ears in the breeds that in some countries have their ears cropped (Boxers, Schnauzers, German breed of Great Dane).

Externally, the ear is massaged with an ointment containing *Echinacea* or *Calendula*.

If contraction of the scar happened some time ago, or if keloids have developed, *Acidum fluoricum 12x*, two doses per day, can be recommended.

Parotid Gland

The parotid gland lies below the ear in dogs. Inflammation (parotitis or mumps) causes this gland to swell and bulge outwards in a lump.

The condition is treated by giving *Pulsatilla 4x* every two hours. If necessary this may after three or four days be followed with *Mercurius solubilis 6x* given several times a day, until the inflammation has completely subsided.

Compresses made with (not too) hot mashed potatoes afford considerable relief to the animal.

As in all cases of illness, the dog will of course be kept indoors and allowed out only to do his 'business'.

If complications such as an accompanying orchitis (or inflammation of the ovary) are noted, *Pulsatilla 4x* is combined with *Arsenicum album 6x*, six times daily each, in alternation.

Brain

Encephalomyelitis (Brain Fever)

The preliminary stage to inflammation of the brain (encephalitis) is engorgement of the blood vessels of the brain with blood. This is observed following extreme exposure to heat, such as sunstroke, or as a preliminary stage in distemper with cerebral congestion, in rabies, or in encephalitis caused by otitis media or an inflammation of the nose spreading to the brain or by metabolic toxins (worms). It should be noted that the disease has become relatively uncommon since the disastrous distemper epidemics after the Second World War, thanks also probably to inoculation against distemper.

The phase of hypersensitivity is marked by excitement, an inclination to bite or to run away, and trembling and even convulsions caused by noise or exposure to light.

At this stage, frequent doses of *Belladonna 4x-6x* are of enormous value, alternating with *Apis 3x* if there are repeated screams or yelps.

The second phase is one of somnolence, uncoordinated movement when walking, the sensitivity getting less, with visual and auditory disturbances, dullness and lack of interest.

The depressive stage responds to *Baptisia 3x*. The drug picture of *Baptisia* has eyelids half paralysed, with very marked reddening of the sclera. The somnolence is quite unparalleled. It should also be mentioned that the tongue is swollen and the mouth filled with saliva which is running from the corner of the mouth.

Gelsemium 6x is the remedy of choice if the pupils are unequal in size, the limbs weak and gait uncoordinated, with the dog trembling.

Encephalitis is a very serious and life-threatening condition. In many cases onset is so vehement that the remedies that are used do not get a chance to act, with death supervening within a short time. It must also be remembered that damaged brain cells cannot be replaced, so that even if the disease is overcome, nervous disorders remain behind that will not respond to treatment.

Stroke (Apoplexy)

Dogs — like human beings — are living to a greater age today. The treatment described below must be given immediately after the stroke if it is to be successful.

The first sign may be convulsions. The dog falls over very suddenly and loses consciousness. The sclera are red, the tongue dark.

The attack may be of short or longer duration, and when it is over, paralysis will be present to a greater or lesser degree.

Treatment consists first of all in isolating the dog in a dark room and keeping him absolutely quiet. He is given *Arnica 3x* alternating with *Belladonna 4x*, initially every fifteen minutes. The drops are given onto the tongue or between the lips. It is only necessary for the medicine to be absorbed into the oral mucosa; it does not have to be swallowed.

As the dog improves, the intervals between doses are increased, as usual.

If the dog remains unconscious for some time, even after treatment with *Arnica* and *Belladonna, Opium 6x* may be tried, every one or two hours. For residual paralysis, see page 117.

A light diet is advisable after apoplexy, giving the dog rusks, milk, gruel, only a little meat, and occasionally a hard-boiled egg.

If there is marked apathy and somnolence, poor memory, dullness and little response to stimulus, it is advisable to follow up treatment with *Helleborus 6x* three times daily and *Baryta carbonica 30x* once a day, both given for some time.

Teeth

Teething

Puppies are born toothless, and the milk teeth are cut at the age of three to four weeks. The permanent teeth begin to erupt in the fourth month, and second dentition is complete by the end of the sixth month. The full permanent dentition consists of forty-two teeth.

Care should be taken not to demand too much of young dogs during the period when the permanent teeth are coming through, not to over-exert them when playing, nor let them get too excited or get a fright. Faulty feeding can lead to complications, the symptoms being fiery redness of the gums, salivation, and a marked pain reaction if the jaws are touched. *Belladonna 4x* given every two hours will easily control these symptoms.

If convulsions occur, *Chamomilla 6x* given at hourly intervals is the remedy.

If the permanent teeth erupt before the milk teeth have been shed, so that both are present at the same time, particularly the canines,*Calcarea phosphorica 6x* should be given four times daily for one month. This is an excellent remedy for correcting disorders in dental development. The milk teeth will be shed naturally, and do not have to be extracted.

The following is a useful course of treatment if one wishes the dog to develop really excellent teeth, with optimum utilization of all good inherited characteristics relating to the bones and teeth.

From the fourth month, 1 tablet three times daily is given of one of the following:

> *Calcarea carbonica 3x*
> *Calcarea phosphorica 6x*
> *Calcarea fluorica 12x*

always changing to another remedy on the next day, the whole for three weeks.

After an interval of two weeks, the same remedies are repeated in a different potency, if required:

Calcarea carbonica 6x
Calcarea phosphorica 12x
Calcarea fluorica 12x

The remedies are also obtainable in powder form.

Premolar defect, a condition known to breeders, will of course not be influenced by this treatment as the tooth buds are missing, a problem due to inbreeding.

Tartar

With age and due to other circumstances, toothache will develop when tartar forms on the teeth and reaches the gums, causing the latter to shrink. Pockets will then develop, with bacteria causing bad smell on the breath and pus around the necks of the teeth. It is necessary to have the tartar removed regularly by a veterinary surgeon.

The best method would of course be to prevent tartar from developing in the first place. This is only rarely achieved however, as the metabolism has to be changed. Tartar consists chiefly of calcium salts precipitated from the saliva which in turn is a product of the fluid metabolism in the organism.

If the constitutional remedy of the animal can be found (see Chapter 17) it should be given occasionally in the 200th potency, to slow down or prevent the development of tartar. If it cannot be found, Tuberculinum 200 may be used as an alternative, a single dose once a month for four to five months. This should at least cause tartar development to slow down.

If the right remedy cannot be found, the worst can be prevented by giving half a teaspoonful of kaolin daily and a cherry-sized piece of baker's yeast once a week, especially if the teeth are also rubbed with lemon juice once a week or cleaned with prepared chalk or one of the commercially available toothpastes for dogs.

It is most important that bones and hard dog biscuits are provided to strengthen the teeth and help to keep them clean. Veal bones are suitable for this, never those from pigs or other bovines. In addition there is one dietary rule that must be strictly adhered to: Not a bite between meals, and never any sweets!

Caries

These measures also help to prevent caries, a condition dogs, and particularly Terriers, are also subject to. It affects predominantly the carnassials and the cheek teeth of the upper jaw. A useful basic treatment in case of caries is *Staphisagria 6x* and *Kreosotum 6x*, 1 tablet four times daily in alternation, for three weeks.

If the dog suffers from suppurative apical periodontitis, an inflammatory reaction that not infrequently develops in the tissues surrounding the root of a tooth, particularly a molar, careful observation will show the animal using great caution in chewing his food, the head is held at an angle, the dog will occasionally rub the painful jaw with his paw, and there may be swelling of the jaw, usually above the molars. In this condition *Pyrogenium 30x* should be given once a day, and *Mercurius corrosivus 6x* three times daily.

If a fistula has already developed from which pus is discharging — an opening will usually be noted beneath one eye — *Silicea 6x*, four times daily, is most likely to help. This applies in the majority of cases where only one root is involved. If however all the roots of a tooth are involved, removal of the tooth under an anaesthetic will be unavoidable.

Periodontosis
Periodontosis, the loss of periodontal tissues around the neck of the tooth, can be treated with *Silicea 4x* and *Natrum phosphoricum 4x*, four times daily in alternation, given for many weeks.

Discoloration of Teeth
Yellow discoloration of the teeth, usually due to distemper or else of unknown origin, might respond to *Silicea 4x*, 1 tablet three times daily, for a number of weeks.

Defects in Enamel
Defects in the enamel may occur if a dog suffers from distemper during the teething period.

Again, *Silicea* is the remedy of choice, given twice daily in ascending potency, each potency for two weeks:
4x – 6x – 10x – 12x.

Loose Teeth
Teeth that have become loose though there is otherwise nothing wrong with them can be made firm again by giving a course of *Argentum nitricum 6x*. This condition will of course only occur at a more advanced age.

Bad Breath

Bad breath, unless due to a great build-up of tartar, calls for *Mercurius sublimatus corrosivus 6x* or *Acidum nitricum 6x*, three or four times daily.

In many cases the offensive smell is due to an eczema of the lips. For the treatment of this, see page 45.

Stomatitis

Poodles in particular are consistently prone to gingivitis and stomatitis (inflammation of the gums and of the mouth generally). Once the condition has become fully established, treatment is usually protracted.

A useful first treatment that has often been found to be rapidly effective is:

> *Belladonna 6x*
> *Echinacea* Mother Tincture

six times daily in alternation.

Lachesis 10x is added if there is blue discoloration at the margins of the mouth or of the ulcer.

Borax 6x is a specific for aphthae.

The course of treatment is concluded with *Sulphur iodatum 4x*, which is given to assist regeneration of the oral mucosa during recovery.

If it becomes necessary to extract teeth where time has taken its toll, *Arnica 6x* should be given several times a day for some days before and after extraction under anaesthesia, with *Hypericum 3x* given several times daily afterwards in addition, for the pain.

When it becomes necessary to extract diseased teeth, there is no point in trying to avoid the procedure. It serves to remove foci of infection that can seriously reduce the general health. The animals are lively and happy again afterwards, as if a heavy mortgage had been taken off their shoulders. The loss of a few teeth is not such a serious matter, for dogs do not normally chew their food very much.

If there was suppuration at the roots of the extraced teeth, *Lachesis 12x* should be given three times daily for two days, to prevent further infection.

Ranula

Ranula (little frog) is caused by inflammation or blockage of a salivary duct through salivary calculi causing a cyst. *Thuja 6x* will restore the condition to normal.

Given in the initial stages, *Thuja* is extraordinarily successful, usually making surgery unnecessary (*Thuja 6x*, five times daily),

Eczema of the Lips

Moist eczema in the fold of the lip, a condition seen particularly in long-haired breeds, is noted for the unpleasant, offensive smell produced by the bacterial flora infecting the lesion. It is sometimes confused with ordinary bad breath.

Treatment with ointments and sprays presents problems, as these are usually licked off by the dog, causing vomiting and gastritis. The dog normally will not permit washing of the area, as the inflammation is extremely painful

Hepar sulphuris 6x is the first remedy to be considered when pain on touch is such that the dog will not permit anyone near the mouth — and this is usually the case. Smell as of old cheese.

The follow-up remedy is *Silicea 6x*, given if there has been no appreciable improvement after some days.

Another remedy that has been useful in this protracted though relatively harmless condition is *Lycopodium 12x*, if the type fits.

The same can be said of *Natrum muriaticum 12x*.

If the smell is extremely offensive, *Kreosotum 6x* has been found effective, three times daily for seven to ten days, at the same time treating the area externally with undiluted *Calendula* tincture.

Rhagades at the Angle of the Mouth

Fissures at the corner of the mouth are occasionally seen nowadays.

Condurango 4x, three times daily, is the remedy of choice, at the same time changing the diet. Hypericum oil is applied externally.

Petroleum 12x has also proved useful in these cases, and *Graphites* for fat dogs.

Epulis

Epulis (the term is applied to any tumour connected with the jaws) tends to occur in several places at once.

If the lesions arise from the mucosa, they are soft and call for *Thuja 6x*.

If they develop from the periosteum, they feel relatively hard and require *Symphytum 2x*.

Tumours originating from the bone, on the other hand, are remarkably hard to the touch. For these, *Hecla lava 6x* together with *Calcarea fluorata 12x* should be given.

The remedies are given for some time, three times daily. The tumours may become stationary, regress, or drop off suddenly. After surgical removal, the remedies will prevent recurrence.

2. Respiratory Tract

Nasal Catarrh, Acute

A simple catarrh with excoriating watery discharge that occurs in conjunction with flow of tears from the eyes and photophobia will quickly respond to *Euphrasia 2x* given several times a day.

Distemper is frequently accompanied by a violent acute catarrh with a bland slimy yellow or yellowy green discharge. In this case, *Pulsatilla 4x* is the remedy.

If the discharge has persisted for some time and is glairy and excoriating, and if there is a tendency to ulceration, *Kalium bichromicum 6x* is required.

A very thick, yellow, viscid discharge calls for *Hydrastis canadensis 6x*. When it is impossible to make the distinction, both remedies may be given in turn, but not more than four times daily. They are also very useful in the treatment of sinusitis.

Watery discharges that are clear like raw egg white and are accompanied by thirst and a dry nose need *Natrum muriaticum 12x*, three times daily, or *Hepar sulphuris 30* for three days, and then *Lachesis 30*, three times daily, for another three days. Purulent sinusitis requires *Hepar sulphuris 6x* and *Cinnabaris 4x* two-hourly in alternation.

Nasal Catarrh, Chronic

When the discharge has become chronic it involves not only the nasal mucosa but also that of the paranasal sinuses and frequently leads to the development of chronic foci of infection.

Good results are achieved by treating with:

> *Kalium bichromicum 4x* and
> *Cinnabaris 5x*

given six times daily for the first few days, and then four times daily, in alternation.

It is essential to maintain close observation of the large intestine, as mucous colitis tends to be present as well (the main indication for this being that the stools are covered with mucus, like a sausage-skin). This must be treated in addition, with the appropriate remedies and a suitable diet (see section on diet, page 64).

Marjoram tea sweetened with a little honey (as a drink) will assist the healing process.

If prior antibiotic therapy has made the bacterial flora resistant, it is best to use the triad:

> *Pulsatilla 30*
> *Hepar sulphuris 30* and
> *Silicea 30.*

Each of these remedies is given for ten days, in the sequence given, preferably as a single dose before going to bed at night. The course of treatment therefore takes thirty days.

Purulent discharge indicates the presence of a foreign body, and this usually requires removal under anaesthesia.

Nose

A dry, cracked nose is indicative of subacute metabolic disorder. *Natrum muriaticum 12x*, three times daily, is the remedy if the diet consists largely of tinned food and the dog is still in the first half of its life.

Older dogs require *Sepia 6x*, three times daily. *Sepia 6x* is also the remedy for changing pigmentation of the nose, when this is light-coloured during summer and dark in winter, and sometimes also changes colour in between times.

A dry, encrusted nose with no cracks should be massaged with cod liver oil. Internally, *Graphites 12x* is given.

An itchy nose calls for *Antimonium crudum 4x.*

Rhagades, fissures and chaps on the wings of the nose are treated with *Petroleum 12x*, those at the base of the nose, on the other hand, with *Alumina 8x.*

When hunting dogs suddenly lose their sense of smell, it is advisable to give them *Phosphorus 6x* for some days. *Natrum muriaticum* may also be considered for this.

Nosebleeds due to mechanical factors are treated by giving *Arnica 3x* every fifteen minutes, and a cold compress applied to the back of the neck. If nosebleeds occur for no obvious reason (or indeed any kind of haemorrhage), *Hamamelis 200* is indicated, once a week.

When the whole family goes down with influenza, it can happen that the four-footed member of the family also catches the infection.

Sneezing, coryza and running eyes, also photophobia and excoriating discharge from the nose, are helped by *Euphrasia 2x*, several times a day. If the remedy is available in high potency, a single dose of the *200* may be given.

Natural remedies, singly or in the combinations some doctors with experience in biological medicine make up for human patients, are also good for animals, for homoeopathy can help all living creatures, and it will cause no harm.

Throat

Tonsillitis, Sore Throat

Sudden difficulty in swallowing and excessive secretion of saliva, frequent yawning, coughing, a red throat with enlarged and inflamed tonsils, pain when the throat is touched, often also reflex vomiting due to narrowing of the throat as the tonsils grow enlarged, loss of appetite, weakness and a raised temperature — these are the signs of tonsillitis, a condition most frequently seen in dogs up to the age of three.

Initially, *Belladonna 6x* is given every one or two hours, later less often as the condition improves. If the condition is getting worse, *Apis 3x* is given two-hourly. If there is no convincing improvement, *Mercurius solubilis 6x* is used, or *Lachesis 12x* if the left tonsil is more inflamed than the right one.

If a tonsillar abscess develops, *Hepar sulphuris 3x* is indicated (as for abscesses generally). A Priessnitz compress also helps: a cold wet compress covered with a woollen scarf and left for two hours.

When tonsillar enlargement persists and proves resistant to treatment, we give *Sulphur iodatum 4x* three times daily for about a fortnight.

Surgical removal of the tonsils is never necessary if the correct homoeopathic treatment is given. I repeat: never. We have never had occasion even to consider it.

Tonsillectomized dogs who became our patients had a tendency to suffer from bronchial conditions. No wonder, as the 'guards at the tonsillar ring' are missing, so that every throat infection immediately moves one stage further down.

A warning must be given that in young animals who have not been vaccinated, tonsillitis may also be the 'virus stage' of distemper.

Laryngitis

Laryngitis may be due to the dog constantly pulling on his lead, or to continuous barking. Other possible causes are a chill caught in spring or autumn, and also in winter through eating snow. Boxers and Pomeranians are most prone to this disease which at a more advanced age, and often in conjunction with bronchitis, makes life difficult for the dog and those around him. It is hard to have to listen to the repeated bouts of coughing, so like asthma, day and night, and the condition generally shows little tendency to improve.

Rapid effective relief of these symptoms is therefore most important. A few doses of *Aconitum 6x* will stop the condition from spreading if there is a cold. These are then followed with *Spongia 6x*, given every two or three hours.

The *Spongia* cough is dry. It develops particularly after excitement and is usually better from eating or drinking.

Goitre

A firm but elastic movable swelling in the region of the pharynx which as a rule does not greatly inconvenience the dog — that is a brief definition of goitre.

If it occurs in young dogs, *Calcarea carbonica 6x* will put a stop to it if the animal is of the *Calcarea carbonica* type: fat, bloated, head heavy, indolent — the lazy dog of popular parlance.

Calcarea iodata is used for dogs that are not of this type, being more lively, and *Calcarea fluorica* for older dogs, where the goitre tends to become malignant.

Emaciated dogs who are losing weight despite a voracious appetite, being extremely restless and nervous and having an excessive need to keep on the move, are given *Iodum 30x* or *Thyreoidinum 30x* once a day.

Lower Respiratory Tract

Cough

A cough has a number of possible causes, and it is most important to have a diagnosis made by the veterinary surgeon.

The bronchitic cough commonly heard after a cold will initially respond to *Belladonna 6x* and *Bryonia 6x* given in alternation. If the cough has already persisted for some days, *Bryonia 6x* and *Tartarus emeticus 6x* are used instead. A Priessnitz compress is always advisable initially, and helps enormously: a wet cold compress around the neck, covered with a woollen scarf, for one or two hours, then rub the neck dry and repeat at night.

The cough caused by pleuritis (see page 52) is treated with *Bryonia* alone.

The cough due to a valvular defect requires cardiac therapy, as the congestion which causes it can only be removed with drugs having cardiovascular action.

Finally, a cough may also be due to pharyngitis or tonsillitis (see page 48). In that case, difficulties in swallowing are the predominant symptom.

A cough due to laryngitis (see page 48) and sometimes also valvular defect calls for *Spongia 6x*. And the cough developing with pneumonia, will respond to the remedies given under that heading.

Kennel cough is an almost epidemic virus disease of several weeks duration that one sees all too frequently. Dogs who have been to a kennel or who have been bought from dealers sometimes have it. *Antimonium arsenicosum 6x* is the remedy of choice, given several times a day.

Bronchitis

Bronchitis usually occurs as the result of a chill, when the mucous membranes lining the bronchial tubes become inflamed. Shortness of breath and attacks of coughing develop, with the cough initially dry, but softer in the later stages.

The rise in temperature is slight. If the temperature does go above 40°C/104°F, distemper may be the likely diagnosis in young animals. A few doses of *Aconitum 6x* given at hourly intervals may check the cough.

Once the bronchitis has gone beyond the intial stage, however, to the point where human patients begin to sweat, whilst dogs will pant, *Belladonna 6x* and *Bryonia 6x* must be given, once an hour in alternation.

The typical *Bryonia* cough is dry, frequent and painful. The dog will therefore lie still and be reluctant to move. The symptoms get worse as he comes into a warm room from outside. In addition he is very thirsty, drinking a lot at one go.

The cough gradually gets easier, it becomes wheezing and then productive. A dog will of course only bring expectoration up to the larynx (there are anatomical reasons for this) and swallow them.

Suitable remedies at this stage are:

   Tartarus emeticus 6x

   Ipecacuanha 6x

every two hours in alternation.

If there is a threat of pneumonia developing, *Tartarus emeticus 6x* needs to be alternated with *Phosphorus 6x*, every two hours.

If there is a marked urge to cough at night, a few doses of *Sticta pulmonaria 2x* or *Drosera 3x* are prescribed in addition.

When the symptoms have died down, *Sulphur 6x* is given to aid final recovery by eliminating all residual toxins. Given three times daily for a few days, it will prevent a relapse.

Dry, Non-productive Cough

This if often due to excitement, triggered not only by fear or shock but also by pleasure (e.g. when greeting members of the family). Dyspnoea with difficulties in taking a breath may be noted — a condition similar to asthma.

The animal is not usually much inconvenienced by this, but the sporadic attacks are somewhat upsetting for those around, especially in older dogs. *Spongia 6x* is of value when even slight pressure on the larynx will trigger an attack.

Arsenicum iodatum 12x is suitable for lean animals who are chilly and show aggravation after midnight. They drink frequently but little, and seek warmth wherever it may be found.

If this does not give results (as happens very occasionally), a combination of:

> *Sulphur iodatum 4x*
> *Stannum iodatum 4x*
> *Tartarus emeticus 6x*

in equal parts is given three to five times daily, half a teaspoonful on the tongue, for some time, less frequently as the condition improves, as usual. This combination has proved its value in both human and veterinary medicine.

Pneumonia

Distemper frequently also involves pneumonia. On the other hand, pneumonia may also be due to a chill or to over-exertion, and in some cases a bad attack of worms or a cough that has been dragging on may be the cause.

The condition starts suddenly, with a high temperature, shivering, trembling, and an increased respiratory rate and pulse. The patient is apathetic and will not touch his food. High temperatures go hand in hand with loss of appetite. Later, a painful cough and mucopurulent nasal discharge develop in addition.

Initially, any condition of this kind, involving high temperatures and an acute vascular situation — rapid respiration, rapid pulse, and in conjunction with this, nervousness and restlessness — can be got under control with a few doses of *Aconitum 6x* given every fifteen, thirty or sixty minutes. If this is not a hundred per cent effective, it is followed with *Belladonna 6x*

Only a very observant owner will usually note this acute stage. When he decides to take the dog to the veterinary surgeon — a decision that is not always spontaneous — this initial stage, which reaches a climax in the evening at around 9 p.m., will already have passed. A good reason for keeping *Aconitum 6x* in the house for your dog! It is a family remedy in the truest sense of the word, but will only effect a cure if given at the beginning of a febrile condition.

Once the Aconitum state has passed, *Aconitum* will have 'lost its bite', exactly because the symptom picture matching the Aconitum drug picture will have disappeared, and a different situation pertains. This also explains why a homoeopathic remedy can only provide the curative regulatory stimulus if it 'fits'. If the wrong remedy has been chosen it will 'miss the mark' and leave no trace, being nontoxic. This is an advantage, compared to other forms of medical treatment, that cannot be estimated too highly. If a few doses of *Aconitum* given at half-hourly intervals have not been thoroughly effective, treatment having started too late, *Belladonna* is given next, in the same way.

If, on the other hand, the pneumonia has already gone through both the *Aconitum* and the *Belladonna* stage, then *Phosphorus 6x* is used in alternation with *Bryonia 6x*. These are the two principal remedies for (catarrhal) pneumonia.

Phosphorus and *Bryonia* medication continues until a productive cough develops, an indication that it is time to change to *Tartarus emeticus 6x*, until recovery is complete.

Antibiotics will not be required in such a case, and progress is much faster.

A dog suffering from bronchopneumonia with severe dyspnoea, taking very short breaths, will typically be nervous and frantically hold up his nose in his efforts to get air, maintaining this position until complete exhaustion. This is the only condition where *Tartarus emeticus* is used earlier, giving it at hourly intervals until there is improvement and then at longer intervals.

If the pneumonia drags on, be it with this treatment or any other, toxoplasmosis must be suspected, tuberculosis, or even lung tumours, which are more common than one likes to think.

Pleurisy (Pleuritis)

The pleura, the serous membrane investing the lungs (pulmonary pleura) and lining the rib cage (costal pleura), easily gets inflamed if there is an infection, with a common cold, or following over-exertion. The condition is always due to the activity of organisms, resulting in pleurisy of the 'dry' (sicca) or of the exudative type.

With the 'dry' type, there is exudation of fibrin on the pleural surfaces, and this causes the characteristic friction rub heard on auscultation. *Bryonia* is the remedy. Even in the most severe cases the symptoms will have disappeared after three days — without any antibiotics or other medication — if *Bryonia 30* is given by subcutaneous injection on the first day and *Bryonia 200* by the same route on the third day.

If the exudate is fluid, this again produces characteristic sounds on auscultation. The amount of fluid may be several litres, usually on one side only, but very rarely so. *Apis 3x* and *Bryonia 6x*, given at hourly intervals, in alternation, will be required.

With both types, breathing is difficult (dyspnoea), superficial and fast, and abdominal respiration will be noted in most cases, with pain when the chest wall is pressed upon.

Tartarus emeticus 6x, three times daily, will deal with any residual cough.

3. Heart

Cardiovascular Remedies

As a dog gets older, the heart grows weaker. This is evident from exhaustion after exertion. Fainting is not uncommon as the condition advances. The organism is able to compensate to some extent for such a failing heart, but it is certainly advisable to give it the necessary support before the condition goes beyond compensation.

There are two homoeopathic remedies that — given together — are highly effective in treating both the ageing heart and cardiac weakness resulting from serious illness.

We use equal parts of *Crataegus 1x* and *Cactus* mother tincture, giving 5-10 drops three times daily.

If cardiac weakness occurs suddenly — febrile infectious diseases can lead to this, with the heart muscle (myocardium) damaged by organisms or their metabolic products, and over-exertion when hunting or coursing is another likely cause – the medication is given every two hours until there is improvement. This acute state is characterized by a strongly beating heart sound, a rapid, barely palpable pulse, dyspnoea, and in conjunction with this cyanosis of the palpebral conjunctiva (membrane lining the eyelids).

Much can be achieved with *Crataegus* and *Cactus*. With older animals, there is the additional advantage that the *Crataegus* component also has a beneficial effect on arteriosclerosis, hardening of the arteries in the brain.

In conditions where the circulation is on the point of failure as in collapse following accidents, *Arnica 3x* and *Veratrum album 3x* are excellent remedies. *Camphora rubini*, 1-2 drops on the tongue every 5-10 minutes, is also promptly effective in all cases of fainting or collapse.

French authors make a finer differentiation. Their recommendations are:

> *Arnica 6x* and
> *Rhus toxicodendron 6x-30x*

for cardiac dilatation, when the dog is apathetic and depressed, only wanting to sit or lie down. One can literally see how heavy his limbs are feeling.

For cardiac hypertropy they advise *Viscum album 3x* and *Cactus 30x*, with *Crataegus 1x* given mainly to treat myocarditis (inflammation of the heart muscle).

They treat endocarditis, the sequel of infectious diseases, focal infection (dentition) and rheumatism in acute cases with:

> *Aurum 30x* and
> *Arsenicum album 6x* or *30x,*

and in chronic cases with:

> *Naja tripudians 6x* or *30x,*

the indication being that the pulse has normal rhythm but varies in strength.

Digitalis 1x is recommended for frank heart failure, when the pulse is slow, oedema is likely to develop, with urinary output decreased. *Strophanthus 1x-3x-6x* should be used if the pulse rate varies between fast and slow, indicating uncompensated mitral insufficiency.

Owners who take good care of their dogs will never allow such serious conditions to develop. A course of *Crataegus/Cactus* therapy or of Crataegutt[1] is begun as soon as there is evidence of heart disease, and continued for at least three months. The heart muscle will need this assistance for that length of time if it is to manage without medication afterwards, providing the damage has not been too serious.

Where heart disease due to old age is more marked, an older animal will of course be given this kind of support for a longer period of time, and some will require it as maintenance therapy to the end of their days.

It might be added that Crataegutt is available also in the form of coated tablets which are more easily taken by some dogs than the drops.

English authors (Biddis) report excellent results with *Cactus 30* in cases where the constrictive pain occurring with angina-type conditions is often taken for a seizure. Dogs clearly also feel the great pain radiating down the left foreleg with sensation of lameness that we know from the description given by humans. They'll instantly raise the extended left foreleg to the level of the ear, the left lip is drawn back, and the animal will usually fall on its right side, something which may happen with older dogs. Three doses of *Cactus 30* at eight-hourly intervals will suffice to prevent further attacks for six months, after which the treament may be repeated if necessary.

[1]A preparation based on extracts of leaves, flowers and fruit of Crataegus marketed by a German firm (Schwabe) - Translator.

4. Digestive Tract

Stomach

Bad Breath

Bad breath may be due to bad teeth. It will be persistent in this case, being due to tartar and hence the development of periodontal pockets, with bacterial flora producing the persistent offensive smell. The only thing that will help here, and is vitally important, is a thorough examination of the teeth, and removal of tartar and rotted teeth where necessary.

All animals given this treatment obviously feel very much better for it, and what is more, they will no longer smell unpleasant. If however the teeth are normal and there is no evidence of tartar, and if oddly enough the smell only becomes offensive at times, it may be concluded that it comes from the stomach on eructation (the gastric mucosa also serve as a safety valve) or from the lungs (gaseous detoxification), and the digestive tract urgently needs to be toned up.

Carbo/Nux therapy is of value here. For about three weeks the dog is given one tablet daily of each of the following:

> *Carbo vegetabilis 6x*
> *Nux vomica 6x*

In chronic cases the course of treatment may be safely repeated after some time.

Kidney disease also causes a sweetish, uraemic breath smelling of urine. The remedies for this are those given under Nephritis (see page 96).

Appetite

Loss of Appetite

This does not refer to the sudden loss of appetite that occurs with acute illness, but rather to the chronic disorder one gets with 'poor eaters'. You may offer the dog whatever you like — he simply does not want it. It requires considerable guile to get him to take even a little. If you try and give him the same the next day, he'll turn his nose up at it. The dog has a capricious appetite, driving everybody to despair.

With this kind of finicky appetite, *Chininum arsenicosum 4x*, three times daily, is a remedy that will soon effect a profound change.

Often, though not always, there is a subclinical liver condition that cannot yet be diagnosed or shown up in tests. The dog appears to have an appetite, for he'll be there the moment he hears the rattle of his food bowl. He takes a real interest in the preparations, jumping up on his mistress and seeming unable to wait to have his meal put in front of him.

When the bowl is finally put down — such a disappointment — he'll just have a mouthful or two, then stop and look around, finally trotting off in disgust, having lost interest. Nothing will then move him to eat any more. A little bit of an appetite will however usually be noted in the evening.

Here, the organism is clamouring for its remedy:

Lycopodium 30, either by injection or 10 granules placed on the tongue.

A single dose will in most cases be sufficient to bring a complete return to normal appetite.

If the appetite only comes with eating, i.e. the dog will only eat once some food has been introduced into his mouth, the indicated remedy is *China 6x*, three to four doses a day.

We all know of dogs who will feed well for some days, but then just as consistently refuse their food. They are otherwise well and happy. Here the remedy is *Ferrum metallicum 5x*, the cause being a problem in iron metabolism. These dogs will also often eat sand.

If the symptoms are less marked, many dogs not doing too well have been helped by the following formula:

  Abrotanum 3x and

  Ferrum phosphoricum 6x

each given three times daily.

A most important factor is a change in diet, particularly for dogs who have become one-sidedly limited to particular foods such as corned beef, kidneys, roast chicken and the like, and refuse to have anything else.

Something needs to be done quickly, to prevent the harmful effects of a one-sided diet, for these are otherwise inevitable.

The best method of introducing a change is a cleansing treatment. This is a treatment that has proved most valuable. To begin with, the dog will fast for three days, when he is given water only, and a mild aperient in the evenings, to empty the gut completely. An empty gut acts like a sponge, absorbing all the toxins in the body that are blocking the normal vital processes.

On the fourth day, the dog is given the following, at the usual time, and well mixed:

> chopped raw meat
> uncooked rolled oats
> grated raw carrots (or another root vegetable
>   that grows below ground)
> chopped raw salad (green leaves, according to season,
>   that have grown above ground)

a tablespoon of each for large breeds, or a teaspoon of each for small breeds.

The quantity is increased by a spoonful of everything per day, until the normal food quantity is reached (the dog will indicate this himself, by leaving some of it). The same diet is maintained for at least four weeks.

This simple treatment has truly miraculous effects and has already helped very many sick dogs. The main advantage is that it does not cost any more than normal feeding. Nature's healing powers will do the rest, if they are allowed to act.

The dog should also have plenty of exercise and access to the open air. It is of great benefit to the patient if afterwards one takes out 'Sickness and Life Insurance for Four-Legged Animals'. This is a precautionary measure that operates under absolutely ideal conditions, insuring the animals against all the harmful effects of overfeeding.

The premium? A day's fasting each week.

What do you get in return? A dog who lives a happy, healthy life right into a ripe old age.

How does one do it? You choose a particular day in the week for the fast, and stick to it.

Your charge will soon realize that there'll be nothing to eat every seventh day, just water to drink. He'll get used to it much more quickly than you think.

Aude sapere - Dare to be wise, dear animal lover and reader.

Depraved Appetite

Puppies as well as adult dogs often have an appetite for things that should not go into a dog's stomach, among them faeces, soil, stones, wood, raw potatoes, carrion and paper. These are signs of a disorder in acid-base metabolism. First of all it is necessary to make sure the problem is not due to worms. If it is, these must be got rid of first (see Worms, page 69). Of course, one should also do something to train the dog so that he does not pick up every bone or whatever looks like food out on the road.

Puppies are helped by a course of *Calcarea carbonica Hahnemannii 6x,* three times daily, if the condition is due to a disturbance of calcium metabolism which is usually the case.

A sign of this is a craving for raw potatoes, and licking the lime wash off the walls.

If the dog also goes for wood or paper, and particularly tissues, *Calcarea phosphorica* is the right remedy to restore calcium metabolism to normal.

A craving for sand is corrected with *Ferrum metallicum 5x.*

Older dogs are given *Carbo/Nux* twice a day when flatus becomes obvious to the ear and the nose and the desire to eat excreta is very marked. A pinch of kaolin should be added to the food in every case.

Baker's yeast, a cherry-sized piece given daily for some time, is just as valuable, having a beneficial effect on the bowel flora.

Sometimes even some smelly cheese will be useful, providing the dog with nutrients he does not otherwise get in his food. If he takes it greedily, one will know how to help him.

An enormous desire to scratch the lime wash off the walls and eat it, and a craving for excreta and indigestible things are the indication for *Acidum nitricum 6x,* given several times a day (possibly also *Alumina 8x).*

A craving for hair points to *Natrum muriaticum 12x* as the remedy.

Vomiting

Simple vomiting of indigestible food is a self-help measure of the organism. Unless repeated, treatment is not really required. If on the other hand vomiting does not cease soon, *Ipecacuanha 6x* is given once an hour, and the animal is made to fast for one day.

The same remedy, *Ipecacuanha 6x,* is very effective when vomiting is due to chemical drugs such as sulphonamides, penicillin, cortisone, etc.

Dogs will often eat grass to induce vomiting. That is a natural desire to correct a problem, and should not be interfered with.

Generally speaking, vomiting is treated as follows:

Vomiting bile in the mornings	*Bryonia 6x*
Vomiting when going by car	*Cocculus 6x*
Vomiting with concusssion	*Arnica 3x-6x*
	Hypericum 2x-4x
Vomiting with gastritis	*Ipecacuanha 6x*
Vomiting after being given chemo- therapy	*Ipecacuanha 6x*
Vomiting with jaundice	*Natrum sulphuricum 6x*
Vomiting undigested food some hours after eating it	*Kreosotum 6x*
Vomiting followed by licking the vomit off the floor or carpet, with excess gastric acid (equivalent to heartburn in man), seen particularly in Boxers	*Acidum sulphuricum 200*

(a single dose on good days, to correct a tendency to the condition, or *Acidum sulphuricum 6x* every fifteen minutes during an attack.)

Vomiting about two hours after a meal, with the vomit immediately eaten, calls for *Nux vomica 6x*.

Vomiting of white mucus in the mornings should lead one to suspect worms (see Intestinal Parasites, page 69).

Gastritis (Inflammation of the Stomach Lining)

Vomiting is the first line of defence, to get rid instantly of the toxins that have caused the gastritis. There are innumerable possible causes: food too cold, too hot or spoiled, contaminated water from ponds or puddles, acrid or excoriating materials the dog has picked up on the road or which have reached the stomach through licking, e.g. if there is a uterine discharge, or rancid oil or fat, frozen grass or snow, and of course also worms.

Lack of gastric acid is indicated by mucus vomited from an empty stomach, and constant desire for certain grasses.

Excess gastric acid will frequently cause vomiting after food.

In both cases, the irritated gastric mucosa responds well to:

Nux vomica 6x and

Pulsatilla 4x

given hourly in alternation until there is improvement.

These two homoeopathic remedies will restore normal composition of gastric acid. A deficit is made up, and an excess reduced.

Gastritis and enteritis are inflammatory conditions affecting the stomach and intestines. One of the two conditions on its own is fairly uncommon, with one usually following the other. If the intestine has become involved, the diarrhoea which occurs is a defensive measure on the part of the organism. It will be followed by loss of appetite, a coated tongue, bad breath, thirst and abdominal pain.

A deep red tongue and prostration, a dog who is restless and nervy, immediately vomiting the little water he has taken, requires *Arsenicum album 6x* every two hours. The Arsenicum picture also includes black diarrhoea in small quantities, possibly thinly streaked with blood.

If the vomiting after a drink of water comes a bit later, so that the water has got warm in the stomach before it was vomited, and if the tongue is red, or coated white, and extremely dry, *Phosphorus 6x* or *12x* will be the remedy.

If the tongue is coated yellow, the oral mucosa is dry, and the dog drinks a great deal at one go, and indeed if hc is also vomiting bile, *Bryonia 6x* should be considered. (*Bryonia* dogs do not run about restlessly, as the *Arsenicum* and *Phosphorus* types do, but prefer to lie still.)

In all these cases, a twenty-four-hour fast should be considered, or better still, fasting until the patient develops an appetite and runs after the person looking after him, being hungry. Even then, only a little, easily digestible food is given, ideally a small amount every four hours, until a return to the normal diet gradually becomes possible.

A Priessnitz compress applied to the chest and abdomen for two hours assists recovery. It helps to relieve pain and also has an antispasmodic effect.

Suitable drinks are weak tea (black), or a mixture of mint and chamomile tea.

Solid food should consist of meat put through the mincer, and cooked pearl barley or rice put through a sieve.

Chronic gastritis is much less dramatic. With this condition, vomiting of undigested food and glassy mucus and a changeable appetite are only rarely seen.

A *Carbo/Nux* therapy will give new tone to the stomach and intestine:
> *Nux vomica 6x*
> *Carbo vegetabilis 6x*

one powdered tablet of each three times daily for two or three weeks.

Diseases of the Pancreas and Spleen

Diseases of the pancreas, if curable, respond well to Harongan[1] (Schwabe), 1 tablet in each food ration, which is then divided into three or four meals. Or one gives *Haronga 3x* for acute pancreatic disorders and *Haronga 4x* for those that have persisted for some time: 5-10 drops three times daily for some weeks.

This plant, found only a few years ago on Madagascar by the well-known physician, chemist and pharmacist Dr Willmar Schwabe, not only makes up for inadequate pancreatic secretion, but also provides a strong curative stimulus for the diseased gland. Again, the interval between doses is increased as the condition improves, gradually phasing the drug out.

Typical symptoms of pancreatic disease are not only continual digestive problems (e.g. irregular appetite, occasional vomiting, changing stools that often have a fatty sheen, voluntary guarding of the abdominal musculature when an attempt is made to palpate the abdomen, with pain evidently felt in the region of the xiphoid process (the small cartilage at the lower end of the sternum), but also the highly characteristic posture: the sick dog stretches his front legs far forward, whilst the hind quarters stay vertically upright. This position clearly affords some relief.

Diabetes (mellitus), or glycosuria, is another form of pancreatic disease. The dog develops an excessive thirst, passing larger quantities of urine than normally. The appetite remains good, but the dog loses condition and gets very thin, as sugar — which normally feeds the tissues — is eliminated in the urine. The diagnosis is always made by a veterinary surgeon.

Before one has to accept the necessity for daily insulin injections, the last resort, it is worth trying the remedies given below. Depending on the severity of the condition, they may help to a greater or lesser extent. One will know whether they are 'hitting the mark' after one week, from the amount of water the dog drinks. This must of course be measured.

The principal remedy is *Syzygium jambolatum 2x*, 10 drops three or four times daily.

The second remedy, specifically for old dogs who are suffering considerable skin irritation with their 'senile diabetes', is *Kreosotum 4x* or *6x*.

Both these treatments are supported by giving *Acidum sulphuricum 12x*.

If the diabetes is not due to deficiency in insulin secretion from the islets of Langerhans in the pancreas, but to injury of the neurohypophyseal system, it is known as diabetes insipidus. This condition is extremely difficult to treat, but an attempt may be made with *Natrum muriaticum 12x* or with the constitutional remedy if this can be found, to try and reduce the dog's thirst and the polyuria to bearable proportions.

Diseases of the spleen are difficult to diagnose. The only indication is usually an increase in girth (X-ray studies and blood tests give valuable assistance towards early diagnosis). All diseases of the spleen are treated with *Ceanothus 1x*.

Loss of Weight

Sometimes a dog will lose weight and condition and become anaemic, though no real cause can be found. It is often impossible to arrive at a clear diagnosis in these cases.

If a course of treatment with:

> *Carbo vegetabilis 6x*
> *Nux vomica 6x* or with
> *Abrotanum 3x*

brings no change, a single dose of *Sulphur 1000* should be tried, particularly if the skin is dry and scurfy, and the dog also suffers from variable stools.

Attention must be paid to diet and plenty of exercise taken.

Loss of weight despite a good appetite and the best of diets, always voraciously hungry (thyroid disorder):

> *Iodum 30x*, once a day.

Loss of weight despite a good appetite in young dogs, with undigested food in the faeces:

> *Abrotanum 3x*, three times daily.

Loss of weight combined with loss of strength:

> *Arsencium album 6x*, three times daily.

Diet

Convenience foods in tins and the various dry dog foods cannot be recommended as the sole items in a perfect diet.

Why not? The preservation process always reduces the vitality of the food, with quality further reduced on subsequent storage. Tinned, dried and frozen foods always take the place of something else – in this case, of fresh food. Fresh food is, and always will be, the very best you can offer, especially to young, growing animals.

Often, dogs do not tolerate certain brands. They will go for the food eagerly and eat it with pleasure, at any time, since chemical attractants have been added. Unfortunately the aroma which has been added also breaks the satiety barrier. The animals in effect no longer know when they have had enough, and will soon gain weight. Fortunately many dogs will then go off the convenience food and refuse to touch it. Others however become 'dependent' and are on the way to developing skin disease, canker and the like, conditions the organism uses as a valve, if it is still functioning normally, to get rid of the toxins.

A meat-only diet is not to be recommended, nor is a meatless diet.

Both will be tolerated, of course, if the dog is trained to them early.

Some vegetarians give their dogs a meatless diet, and the dogs manage, despite the fact that nature has given them the teeth and the short gut of a carnivore (herbivorous animals have a long gut).

Volumes have been written on the feeding of dogs. There are many different views and innumerable diets have been proposed. Let us not add to the collection, but merely state briefly that very many patients who have had the cleansing treatment prescribed (see page 59) were then kept on this diet because they did so well on it, and have lived to a ripe old age without ever getting seriously ill again or needing to be seen by a veterinary surgeon.

That is a clear indication of a well-balanced diet, such as:

1 part raw meat
1 part cereal grains and
2 parts plant food

These patients were mostly around the middle of their life span, and it is an excellent diet for the second half of life.

Generally speaking, the following is a useful formula:

> For the first eighteen months of its life, until it reaches adulthood, a dog is given 2 parts of meat, 1 part of cereal and plant food,
>
> adult dogs require 1 part of meat and 2 parts of cereal and plant food,
>
> from the seventh year onwards, as the dog is getting older, he needs 1 part of meat, 1 part of cereal grain, and 2 parts of plant food.

This applies to all dogs who are not working, i.e. are not hunting dogs, police dogs etc., and therefore lead the normal 'dog's life'. With older dogs it must be taken into account that with advanced age the dog becomes less able to degrade proteins in his digestion down to the last stage. This final stage is urea, a substance that is easily eliminated via the kidneys. The last-but-one stage is uric acid, which is not eliminated easily. Protein degradation impaired by old age or by other causes stops at this stage, with the result that the uric acid is deposited in the muscles and other organs and illnesses arise. It is first of all deposited in the lumbar musculature, which is immediately obvious from the swelling of the affected region and pain on light pressure. The animals will sit down immediately if gentle pressure is applied to the area. They are far from their usual happy selves, no longer leaping about, and stairs, too, are a problem (uric acid diathesis).

Reducing the amount of meat in the diet as the dog gets older will therefore always extend life. It is always possible to increase the protein content by adding milk products (protein from a living animal) which are just as nourishing but more easily tolerated (low-fat soft cheese, yoghurt); also eggs.

Unless you are very keen to feed your dog according to the rules, or on a particular system, and if you also do not think very much of convenience foods, then you'll feed your dog the way it has been done for thousands of years — on what man gives him of his own food, sharing the food of man.

If this means a variable diet that is not too highly seasoned, such a diet will be well tolerated, in spite of what the advertisements say.

Liver

Liver Disease

The following is a general principle: if putrefaction occurs in the intestine, toxins are produced that damage the surface of the gut and enter into the bloodstream. The veins from the duodenum carry these toxins to the liver, where they are detoxicated. Even a minor ailment affecting the gut always imposes a considerable strain on the liver. If detoxication is not complete, the liver itself becomes damaged, and we get the loss of appetite seen on recovery from enteric disease.

In most cases, however, liver damage is due to external factors, be it the ingestion of rat poison, or poisoning from bacteria and their toxins, unsuitable worm treatments and other chemotherapeutic measures — all of them equally bad.

Dogs generally tend to suffer from liver damage with no clearly definable symptoms. All one notices is a certain lassitude, and that the dog is drinking surprisingly little, is very tired, and keeps yawning a great deal.

It may be several days before yellow, bilious mucus is vomited. *Chelidonium* is useful for this mild type of condition, particularly if given in high potencies, to stimulate, in a way, the nerve centres responsible for hepatic function and restore this to normal: *Chelidonium 30*, two or three times daily until the condition improves.

Acute hepatitis (inflammation of the liver) shows itself by vomiting and diarrhoea (or constipation) and severe pain if pressure is applied in the liver region. The dog is weak and apathetic, and the urine is very dark. Jaundice may develop on occasion.

Acute hepatitis may become chronic, though the chronic form also occurs on its own in older animals. The cause is toxins produced due to metabolic deficiencies. The condition gradually progresses into cirrhosis of the liver. This is a condition that takes a long time to develop to its final stage, and it is difficult to identify: initially changeable appetite and digestive disorders, later emaciation, circulatory disorders and ascites.

One's first concern must be to relieve the strain on the liver by giving a suitable diet. A liver-protective diet for a dog (unless the veterinary surgeon prescribes a ready-made-up diet food) will contain little meat or fat, plenty of carbohydrates such as cereal products, rice and other gruel, glucose in the food or in the drinking water, and mint tea.

The second step is to choose the right remedy. Dr Wolter, my colleague in Ottersberg, has been able to do a trial on a liver remedy that has a specific broad-band action, testing it on pigs. *Flor de Piedra* will help the liver to regenerate rapidly, a remedy of inestimable value to all animals and of course also to man.

We give *Flor de Piedra 3x*, one tablet several times a day, until the condition improves.

For chronic liver conditions, the following treatment has proved effective:

Lycopodium 30	one dose the first evening
Nux vomica 30	one dose the second evening
Phosphorus 30	one dose the third evening,

i.e. the three remedies in alternation, daily at first, and every second or third day as the condition improves.

Jaundice

The causes of jaundice are numerous, but it must always be considered a very serious symptom. It is not a disease as such, but indicates that there is an obstruction to the flow of bile from the gall bladder.

The most common causes are infectious diseases such as Stuttgart disease or infectious hepatitis, or poisons that destroy hepatic tissue, such as phosphorus, arsenic, chloroform, pharmaceutical products, bacteria, toxins. Diseased liver cells are unable to secrete bile into the small intestine. Bile pigments and acids therefore enter the blood, and if present in sufficiently high concentration cause the yellow coloration of the skin and mucous membranes known as jaundice.

This does of course have a major effect on the general health, resulting in tiredness, loss of appetite, vomiting and diarrhoea, stools that are grey and clayey because the bile pigments are missing, and cardiovascular symptoms. The urine is dark, and all the mucous membranes — eye, mouth, penis, anus — are yellow.

Treatment is determined by the cause. In the case of an epidemic, antibiotic therapy will be required.

A useful homoeopathic remedy is *Natrum muriaticum 6x*, once an hour throughout the day, and less frequently as the condition improves.

Chelidonium and *Taraxacum 4x-6x* may be given to support this treatment.

Intestines

Constipation

Constipation is always due to lack of exercise or lack of balance in the diet, unless the dog suffers from a serious condition such as enlargement of the prostate, a hernia, or tumours in the visceral region.

Lack of exercise and of a balanced diet must be corrected. A change of diet is an initial requirement with any form of treatment, and it is also essential to make sure the dog gets enough air and exercise.

In mild cases of acute constipation, a few doses of *Nux vomica 6x* are given every one or two hours, or some teaspoons or tablespoons of castor oil every two hours, until the dog is able to pass a motion. (Dogs require more castor oil than humans.)

If on the other hand the dog has had too many bones, and there is not enough gastric acid to decalcify them and make them digestible, stone-hard bone stools are formed in the colon. Their removal will only be possible with the aid of a veterinary surgeon, unless warm water enemas solve the problem.

Chronic constipation in older dogs requires *Alumina 8x* when great effort on their part gives no result.

If peristalsis has ceased completely and the intestine seems paralysed, *Opium 6x* is the remedy of choice.

Spasms in the anal sphincter, with tenesmus (violent and ineffective straining) and constipation due to too many medicinal drugs call for *Nux vomica 6x*.

For spasm of the anal sphincter with hard black balls like sheep's dung or crumbly yellowy motions, *Magnesia phosphorica 6x* is given.

Disorders of intestinal secretion, with the mucosa very dry, great thirst, large calibre motions in the form of large balls, dry and hard, as if burnt, need *Bryonia 4x-6x*.

If every motion looks different from the one before, or the dog is constipated one day and has diarrhoea the next, this is an indication for *Pulsatilla*.

Constipation and diarrhoea in one and the same motion is a symptom calling for *Sulphur 6x*.

Constipation always indicates an underlying intestinal weakness.

It is therefore advisable to restore normal tone to the stomach and intestines with that excellent combination:

Nux vomica 6x

Carbo vegetabilis 6x

1 tablet of each three times daily for three weeks.

Colic (Meteorism)

Colic is uncommon in dogs, though sometimes seen in Dachshunds. If it does occur, it is a serious condition, with pain, restlessness, whining and barking or, depending on the temperament, standing silently in a corner, the abdomen tucked up and tensed. It will be bloated like a barrel and as rigid as a board.

With the dog also unable to walk, the condition may indicate the onset of paralysis due to changes in the nucleus pulposus, a disease mostly seen in Dachshunds.

Colocynthis 3x or *Magnesia phosporica 6x* given every fifteen minutes will however make these symptoms disappear rapidly.

It will then be necessary to restore a normal intestinal flora by giving *Asafoetida 4x* and *Nux vomica 4x,* three times daily, and in addition a weekly dose of *Lycopodium 200.*

Intestinal Parasites

Intestinal parasites harm the host animal in three ways:

They cause damage to the intestinal mucosa (mechanically and chemically), their excretions are a nerve poison, and they share the host's food, especially if present in large numbers. The result tends to be unthrifty pups with distended abdomens.

The safest way of ridding young organisms of these parasites is homoeopathic treatment with a remedy like *Abrotanum 2x-3x* (or *Cuprum oxydatum nigrum 4x*) which changes the intestinal environment, thus forcing the worms to depart as the situation is no longer tenable for them. The treatment is continued for seven days, giving *Abrotanum 3x* to puppies, and *Abrotanum 2x* to older dogs. The dose is 1 tablet or 10 drops given with food, at least three times daily.

The worms will be passed on the seventh, eighth or ninth day at the latest. It is not surprising to see them still mobile in the motions, for they have not been poisoned. We have simply made the gut able to rid itself of the parasites, a big difference from the usual worms treatments.

This treatment avoids additional damage to the organism from chemicals. A weekly dose of *Calcarea carbonica 200* will protect the patient from a renewed invasion of worms. Duration of treatment: four weeks.

Occasionally there is a dog who in spite of every chemical treatment does not get rid of his worms and has the parasites for months and even years.

In a case like this, *Calcarea carbonica 200* (or higher) again shows its alterative effect, changing the intestinal environment and preventing infestation with worms, even tapeworms.

If a dog has tapeworms, these are got rid of with a safe chemical tapeworm treatment, making sure at the same time that the dog no longer has fleas, which act as intermediate hosts.

Calcarea carbonica 200 as a follow-up treatment will enhance the body's own defences against intestinal parasites, including tapeworms. Duration of treatment: four weeks.

Foods high in vitamin A are of great value at this time, e.g. cod liver oil, grated carrots, egg yolk, milk and fish.

Enteritis

The chief symptom is diarrhoea, with the stools pultaceous (mushy) or watery, slimy or even mixed with blood.

Dogs who are in good condition are made to fast and given the appropriate remedy. Dogs in a reduced state of health need a diet with certain restrictions: no fat, no milk, no sugar, no vegetables and no bones. Gruels made from rice or pearl barley should be given, and weak tea or a mixture of chamomile and mint tea. If necessary a small quantity of rusk may be broken into the tea. During the days that follow, lean meat put through the mincer, meat broth without fat, an egg and a little boiled fish may be given, depending on the dog's condition.

One then looks at the diarrhoeic motions, for it is these and the way they are produced that serve as the indication for the remedy. Nature's own language — the presenting symptoms — needs to be translated into the right homoeopathic remedy.

Pulsatilla 4x-6x is useful with all slimy diarrhoeas, when no motion resembles the one before, each being a different colour and different in appearance, but always slimy. The cause here is intolerance of foods containing too much fat, and also of fruit.

Podophyllum 4x is known as the remedy for 'hydrant' stools that gush from the anus to quite some distance, particularly in the mornings and after a feed (enteritis involving the duodenum). They are watery, painless and putrid.

Mercurius solubilis 4x is considered the remedy if the motions are white or yellowy and contain some blood, and there is much straining, as if the dog would never be finished.

Sulphur 6x is used when there is diarrhoea only in the early morning, and none at all during the day.

Arsenicum album 6x is the remedy for diarrhoea with rapid emaciation and exhaustion. The motions are frequent but small in quantity, with a cadaverous smell and sometimes mixed with blood. The animal takes quite frequent drinks, but only a little at a time (very important). The water is usually vomited again. The tongue is dry and red. There is a peculiar aggravation after midnight, with fear and restless running to and fro, also motions passed at night. Better from warmth, so that these patients will not move away from the radiator.

Arsenicum album 6x is indicated if the diarrhoea has been caused by poisoning due to bad food, bad boiled meat, fish or meat products which dogs tend to pick up in the street. It is a useful remedy for any form of poisoning, and for diarrhoea after eating ice or very cold drinks, cold food straight from the refrigerator, frozen grass and also snow.

Chronic enteritis, when diarrhoea alternates with constipation, calls for *Antimonium crudum 4x*.

If there is both diarrhoea and constipation in one stool, *Sulphur 6x* is the remedy of choice. If the stool is coated with mucus (like a sausage skin), *Mercurius sublimatus corrosivus 12x* or *Aethiops antimonialis 4x* is indicated (mucous colitis).

Graphites should also be mentioned, for a colitis where the dog is constipated for days. This may be seen in dogs of the Graphites type – overweight, disinclined to move, and always hungry (see Graphites Type, Chapter 17).

Orthodox medicine is rather inclined to 'stop' any diarrhoea with a powerful drug, yet diarrhoea provides an excellent example of the very individual approach to the choice of a remedy by the homoeopath. He has to consider the different symptoms as well as the whole picture, taking into account also the triggering factor.

Diarrhoea after milk	*Calcarea carbonica*
Diarrhoea mornings only, not during the day	*Sulphur*
Diarrhoea in the afternoons	*China*
Diarrhoea at night	*Arsenicum album*
Diarrhoea immediately after a feed	*China, Pulsatilla*
Diarrhoea after getting wet through	*Rhus toxicodendron*
Diarrhoea after a chill	*Dulcamara*
Diarrhoea weakens and exhausts	*Chininum arsenicosum*

Diarrhoea from fear	*Gelsemium, Argentum nitricum*
Diarrhoea after travelling for some time	*Cocculus*
Chronic diarrhoea	*Sulphur 30*, twice daily.

Choice of potency: *6x-30x*, depending on the case.

If there is residual weakness of the sphincter, with the dog passing stools without noticing it (which should not be punished, of course), *Causticum 12x* or *Aloe 12x* three times daily for a few days will soon help.

Anal Glands

The anal glands which are situated on either side of the rectum produce an offensive secretion that serves as a 'scent marker'. This is normally secreted into the rectum when there is pressure as a motion is passed.

If the efferrent ducts are blocked, the glands become inflamed and the dog 'goes tobogganing'. He drags himself along the ground (usually thought to be due to worms), and licks the anus thoroughly if able to reach it. He will often throw his head back suddenly, as though he felt a lancinating pain. This stabbing and radiating pain from the inflamed glands can be so violent that it causes temporary lameness. The anus appears reddened and swollen on one side, rarely on both. An abscess will frequently develop.

In the latter case, we apply the usual treatment for an abscess (see Chapter 9): *Hepar sulphuris 3x* every two hours until the abscess bursts spontaneously, followed with *Silicea 12x* twice a day to complete the cure.

If there is no abscess, but merely redness and irritation of the anus and surrounding areas, *Aesculus 3x*, four or five times daily, will help, with *Hamamelis* ointment applied externally.

If the dog is also suffering from constipation, *Nux vomica 6x* is given four times daily in addition.

Chronic inflammation of the anal glands, with no abscess forming, requires *Silicea 30* and *Echinacea 30*, both given twice daily for two weeks.

Constantly suppurating anal glands are an indication for *Calcarea sulphurica 12x*, three times daily for the first, and twice daily for the second week.

Hamamelis suppositories introduced into the rectum at night, when the last motion has been passed and before going to sleep, are very helpful.

In very small dogs, where suppositories cannot be used, massaging the anus with *Hamamelis* or *Calendula* ointment will help. Another useful measure is a sitz bath with 4 teaspoons of tincture of *Calendula* or *Hamamelis* to $\frac{1}{4}$ litre of warm water.

Anal Disease

Anal fissures respond well to *Acidum nitricum 12x*.

Anal fistulas require *Silicea 12x,* or *Acidum nitricum 12x,* or *Calcarea fluorica 12x.*

Anal eczema is treated either with *Acidum nitricum* or *Petroleum 12x.*

Suppuration in the anal region calls for *Calcarea sulphurica 6x* or *12x,* several times a day.

Anal prolapse is corrected with a purse-string suture, after which *Ruta 3x* and *Ignatia 6x* are given.

Anal tumours are often helped by *Arsenicum iodatum 6x,* given three times daily for some time, or by *Acidum fluoricum 12x* twice daily in a case of varices.

[1]350 mg tablets containing 2.5 mg of Extr. Harongae — Translator

5. Locomotor System

Muscles

Strain
Dogs who have become 'dog-tired' after very long walks or from running should immediately be given *Rhus toxicodendron 30* or *Acidum lacticum 30* after such over-exertion, to prevent muscle pain.

Muscular Rheumatism
Dogs of any age – but older ones obviously more so – are liable to suffer from this disease which occurs more often in summer than in winter. The rheumatism may affect the muscles of the neck. The animal will then cry out as soon as small muscle groups go into spasm, irrespective of whether he is moving or not. The neck appears both shorter and thicker. Dachshunds and Bassets are particularly liable to this condition.

Belladonna 6x, an hourly dose to begin with, and less frequently as the condition improves, will help in these cases. If elderly bitches have the disease, *Cimicifuga 6x* will be more useful, as the cause is usually hormonal, and hormonal balance is restored by *Cimicifuga*.

If the back of the neck is involved, wry-neck (torticollis) may develop, with the head constantly held to one side. French authors recommend *Lachnanthes tinctoria 6x* and *Phosphorus 12x* in these cases, but *Rhus toxicodendron 30* and *Bryonia 30* given in alternation will also hit the mark.

The lumbar and sacral region may be very seriously affected (lumbago). The dog then shows lameness, moving with enormous effort without standing up completely on his hind legs, and there may be complete lameness for a time.

Recovery is rapid with *Bryonia 6x-30x* and *Rhus toxicodendron 6x-30x* given once an hour in alternation and less frequently as the condition improves. Another useful treatment is a weekly injection of *Acidum formicicum 30*. This deals with the predisposition to rheumatism.

A dry, warm bed free from all draughts is essential for recovery, and concrete-lined kennels must also be avoided if there is to be an improvement.

Symptoms developing after an awkward jump or other unnatural movement that are very painful are treated with *Rhus toxicodendron 12x* every two hours, until the pain has gone.

Shaking Palsy

This is a condition affecting particularly Terriers and Schnauzers. The trembling of the limbs tends to persist throughout the day, except when the dog is walking, and ceases in sleep.

> *Magnesiam phosphorica 6x*, three times daily on the
> first day, and
> *Kalium phosphoricum 6x*, three times daily on the
> second day,

continuing like this for some time, will prove very useful, particularly if *Gelsemium 200* is given in between, every tenth day.

It can also happen that dogs, and particularly Poodles, begin to shake like a leaf when being trimmed or on the examination table. The trembling will not stop even when all four paws are held. Once they are off the table and walking in the road, there is not a trace of a tremor.

This is a condition due to fear, the *Argentum nitricum* fear. Given in the 12th potency, a single dose each night, this remedy will cure the condition in a few weeks.

Ligaments, Tendons, Joints

Ligaments torn off the bone require the same remedies as bone fractures:

> *Calcarea phosphorica 6x* and
> *Symphytum 3x* in alternation.

LM potencies are even more effective than the low potencies. They will 'weld' the ligament to the periosteum (12th, 15th, 18th *LM*). Five drops three times daily, after shaking the bottle ten times.

Lax joints are quite often seen in Alsatians. The dog stands at too acute an angle to the ground, indicative of connective tissue weakness. This is easily corrected with the connective tissue remedy *Calcarea fluorata 12x*, three times daily for a number of weeks. A weekly dose of *Silicea 200* is given in addition.

Sprains

A sprain is a temporary displacement of joint surfaces which then immediately return to their original position. It is caused by slipping, stumbling, missing a step, a limb getting caught, and similar accidents.

The situation is usually complicated by the presence of effusions (haematomata), considerable stretching and even tearing of a ligament causing lameness, and sensitivity and swelling in the area.

Local treatment consists of:

> Compresses using *Arnica* mother tincture, 25 drops to a glass of water, or massaging with *Kytta Fluidbalsam*[1] twice daily for five minutes.

> Internally, *Arnica 3x* and *Rhus toxicodendron 8x* are given in alternation every one or two hours.

If a torn ligament is suspected, or injury to the periosteum, *Ruta graveolens 4x* is given in addition, dispensing the three remedies as a mixture, first hourly, and then, as the condition improves, every two hours, for several days.

Tenovaginitis (Inflammation of Tendon Sheath)

The following will be found useful in the treatment of tenovaginitis:

> *Arnica 4x*
> *Ruta graveolens 3x*
> *Rhus toxicodendron 8x*

in equal parts, every two or three hours to begin with, and after improvement three times daily, until the cure is complete.

Massaging the area with *Kytta Fluidbalsam* twice a day for a full five minutes is an excellent supportive measure, or also *Kytta Plasma* compresses (see note at end of chapter).

Arthritis

Inflammation of the joints, be it acute or chronic, is due to many different causes that are either traumatic or infectious. There is generally a marked lameness, or even inability to put the affected limb to the ground.

The limb should be immobilized, and treatment given as follows:

Belladonna 4x-6x if there are marked signs of inflammation such as swelling, heat, redness, pain, lameness and perhaps also a raised temperature. The remedy is given at short intervals, every one or two hours, and less frequently as the condition improves.

Bryonia 6x is the remedy for swollen joints where the slightest movement is causing pain. Better from firm pressure, so that the patient is lying on the affected joint. The dog will also drink a great deal at one go, though not frequently, a peculiarity of Bryonia that in this case is the absolute indication for the remedy.

Rhus toxicodendron tends to be indicated for inflammation of ligaments and tendons, with aggravation from rest, so that the first movements after getting up with difficulty are painful and much trouble. After just a few steps the situation improves and the dog 'gets going', though later on he will again find it harder to walk. *Rhus toxicodendron 30*, three times daily, is a reliable remedy in these cases.

If there are no clear indications for either *Bryonia* or *Rhus toxicodendron*, both remedies may be given every two hours in alternation.

Massaging the joint with *Kytta Fluidbalsam* (see note at end of chapter) twice daily for five minutes is also helpful.

Chronic arthritis has a good chance of recovery if weekly injections of *Phosphorous 30* are given subcutaneously or intracutaneously, above the joint, by a veterinary surgeon. A series of four injections has been found effective.

Tendency to Dislocate Joints

A tendency to dislocate joints and knee ligaments, i.e. their temporary displacement which causes complications with walking, is treated with:

Rhus toxicodendron 12x in the mornings and

Chamomilla 6x at night

for three or four weeks.

A repetition of this treatment some time later will often be indicated.

Bones

Rickets

Rickets has become a rare condition nowadays, as dogs, and particularly pregnant bitches, are generally fed and cared for more efficiently. The disease affects puppies and bitches after whelping.

The first sign is usually that the animal is constantly licking the walls. The hip and knee joints remain soft and do not calcify and, like the other bones, are deformed under the influence of the weight of the body. Bow legs, a dropped back, enlarged carpal joints and 'bear's paws' are the consequence.

Swellings also appear at the points where the ribs join their rib cartilages, a phenomenon to which the name of a 'rosary' has been applied.

The causes are not only incorrect feeding of the dam, but also lack of fresh meat, exercise, sunlight, light and fresh air. Severe infestation with worms may also be the cause. If treatment is given early, much can be achieved. In most cases, recovery progresses so well that one does not recognise the animals again when they have been on the treatment for some time.

A change of diet to include raw meat is just as important as giving raw milk, raw eggs, cod liver oil, a mixture of mineral salts, and an intensive course of vitamin D, for about ten days in the month.

The sick animal needs to be played with a great deal, and to be out in the open, in plenty of fresh air and sunlight.

The imbalance in calcium metabolism is treated with:

Calcarea phosphorica 3x
Calcarea carbonica 6x

1 tablet of each three times daily.

Developmental Disorders

In principle it can be said that imbalance in mineral metabolism is responsible for the bone changes that have been increasingly in evidence in our dogs in recent years.

Every dog food manufacturer has a different concept of mineral metabolism, but the overall result is a constant oversupply, so much so that many organisms cannot cope with it. Changes in bone structure or deposits are the result, putting the dog on the road to outright illness.

Calcarea carbonica
Calcarea fluorica
Phosphorus

and other remedies prescribed according to the law of similars will restore mineral metabolism to normal, saving the need for surgery and other expensive manipulations.

A number of disorders diagnosed under names such as osteofibrosis or spondylitis, diffuse bone contours in X-ray pictures, inexplicable lameness in puppies and also in adults dogs can in many cases be improved or at least helped functionally with

Calcarea carbonica 30x or
Calcarea fluorica 30x, depending on the type.

The X-ray picture will not change to any appreciable degree, but the patient feels well and functions normally.

Many an old Dachshund who has had repeated attacks of lameness ought no longer to be able to walk according to his X-rays, but he still can nevertheless.

Fractures

Fractures require *Calcarea phosphorica 6x* and *Symphytum 3x,* four times daily in alternation.

These two remedies will lead to rapid callus formation. *Symphytum* is always indicated with bone injuries, *Ruta* if the periosteum only has been damaged.

The muscular atrophy due to immobilisation disappears rapidly with *Plumbum 6x* given three times daily.

Abnormalities of Nails

Abnormalities of the nails frequently result in repeated removal of the nail, without having affected the cause.

Antimonium crudum 4x is a marvellous remedy for nails that grow distorted and are cleft.

Silicea 6x may be tried for crippled nails, *Thuja 6x* for brittle and cracking nails, and finally *Graphites 4x* for thickened, crippled nails in animals with the familiar *Graphites* constitution: 'fat, stupid, indolent, depressed, chilly and constipated', and for dry skin tending to fissure.

The chronic metabolic disorder that lies at the back of this requires treatment for an extended period of several weeks. *Sulphur 30* given intermittently after the second week, to stimulate reaction, is useful in these cases.

Dew Claws

Dew claws should be removed on the first day of life, with a short sharp cut of the scissors, and not later on in life, when local or general anaesthesia will be required.

During the first three days of life, no real sensation of pain has yet developed, and the dam will lick the wound afterwards to assist healing.

It is not the custom to remove dew claws from the forelegs as well, but it is advisable, for these claws often grow into the flesh, or the dog may hurt himself when scratching.

---

[1] A compound containing extracts of Symphytum, Arnica etc. – Translator.

6. Male Sex Organs

Balanitis

A discharge from the male sex organ of a dog tends to be an annoyance to the owner. The dog is licking the part because it is burning, and is constantly shedding drops of thick, yellow pus, though this may also be thin and excoriating and have a very offensive smell. The condition is due to bacterial infection of the prepuce and of the terminal part of the urethra.

The inflammation of the mucosa is not life-threatening, but treatment tends to be difficult and protracted, as antibiotics do not generally help. What is required in these cases is alteration and improvement of the terrain, restoring the mucosae to health, so that these bacteria are unable to thrive on them.

For hygienic as well as aesthetic reasons, it is well worth the trouble to deal with the situation.

The following have proved effective:

Mezereum 3x for balanitis occurring in conjunction with urethritis; the discharge comes mainly from the urethra; three or four doses daily.

Pulsatilla 3x for a thick, greeny yellow discharge that does not cause soreness, being bland.

Mercurius solubilis 6x if the discharge causes soreness; there may be small ulcerations in the mucosa.

Hepar sulphuris 6x for a copious discharge that does not irritate but — as one would expect with this remedy — smells of old cheese.

Silicea 12x if none of the above apply and the discharge has been there 'for ever', i.e. has become chronic.

An excellent solution for bathing the mucosae is made by adding 1 teaspoon of *Calendula* or *Echinacea* tincture to a glass of water.

Neoplasms on the Penis

Neoplasms on the penis taking the form of warts are occasionally seen. *Thuja 6x*, four times daily, is the remedy of choice.

If there are secretions with striking offensive smell, even stinking, and the warts are highly sensitive to touch and bleed easily, *Acidum nitricum 6x*, four times daily, is required.

Eczema of the Testicles

Eczema of the testicles — not to be confused with orchitis — involves the skin of the testicles and not the testicle as such.

The specific remedy for this is *Croton 6x* given internally four times daily.

This is instantly effective, and better than all corticoid preparations and ointments which dogs tend to lick off, causing them to vomit.

If vesicles have formed, a dose of *Rhus toxicodendron 30x* is given at night in addition.

Orchitis

Orchitis (inflammation of the testicles) is usually due to mechanical injuries resulting in bruising and contusions. We have however also seen it after parotitis.

Orchitis is extremely troublesome and the dog walks with difficulty. The testicle is swollen and painful, in contradistinction to tumours of the testicle which develop gradually, increasing slow'*y* in size, without causing any particular pain. Fever and apathy complete the picture.

If there has been bruising, *Arnica 6x* given at short intervals will help.

If there is redness and the testicles feel hot, *Pulsatilla 6x* is also required. The follow-up remedy, if indicated, is *Spongia 6x*.

Chronic inflammation of the testicle, usually due to a tumour, is treated with *Conium 6x* if hard in consistency, and otherwise with *Thuja 6x*. Castration will only rarely be necessary.

Calcarea iodata 6x is another excellent remedy; with *Conium* and *Thuja* it forms the triad of remedies for glandular tumours.

Unilateral inflammation calls for *Clematis 4x* for the right testicle, *Rhododendron 6x* for the left.

Local compresses with *Hamamelis*, using a suspensory T-bandage to envelop and support the painfully inflamed scrotum, will be a help with large dogs. The epididymis is of course always involved too.

Prostate

Prostatitis

Acute inflammation of the prostate is easily confused with lameness in the hind quarter, particularly in Dachshunds. Considering the descriptions given in human cases, this is not surprising, for the patients complain of a sensation of a burning ball between the thighs, painfully felt at every step. This is also why no dog is keen to walk when his prostate is inflamed, and if he has to, does so with legs apart and rather clumsily. Jumping and going on stairs are out of the question. Sensitive animals will give a sudden blood-curdling yelp when they are trying to stretch.

The gland, normally about the size of a plum, depending on the breed, reaches the size of an apple. When massaged by the veterinary surgeon, it is so painful that most dogs will cry out. However, the pain lessens whilst this treatment is still in progress, and when the patient jumps off the table and finds himself on solid ground once more, he is visibly pleased, jumping and barking and wagging his tail. This is a good sign, as it confirms the diagnosis.

Acute prostatitis is initially best treated with *Belladonna 6x* and *Pulsatilla 3x-6x*, once an hour in alternation. When the inflammation has gone down after some days, *Bryonia 6x* is given for a few days, three times daily. One may of course also follow with *Thuja 6x*.

Hyperplasia (Enlargement) of Prostate

This may later develop into an adenoma or even a malignant tumour. Enlargement of the prostate occurs in old dogs even when there has been no prior disease. *Pulsatilla 30* is the remedy of choice. Given in the morning, at midday and at night for seven days, it will rapidly bring relief. It is advisable to repeat the treatment one month later.

Oedema of the Prostate

Prostatic oedema is the diagnosis if the soft, enlarged gland goes down in size with amazing rapidity when massaged with the forefinger. It is a condition fairly frequently seen in hunting dogs. *Digitalis 1x* is used to treat what is in effect a vascular problem, giving it three or four times a day until the prostate has returned to normal.

Induration of the Prostate

If the gland has already hardened and become enlarged (adenoma), *Conium 6x* is the remedy if the hindquarter is insecure or weak and there is increased thirst, or *Thuja 6x* if there is insatiable hunger.

The magnesium salts, *Magnesia carbonica 12x*, *Magnesium chloratum 12x* and *Magnesia phosphorica 12x*, are indicated when the above symptoms are not present.

These remedies need to be given for three weeks.

Operations on the prostate are also done in veterinary surgery, but they become unnecessary if the above treatments are used. It is so often the case that homoeopathic treatment makes surgical intervention unnecessary. In thirty years of practice, for instance, with a large number of patients, tonsillectomy has not once been necessary.

Sexual Urge (Libido)

Excessive Libido

Both sexes make their sexual desires extremely clear. Males roam around and become excited at the scent of every bitch on heat. Bitches in turn exhibit their typical behaviour, against the crossed legs of their master or any visitor.

It is possible to regulate the hormonal imbalance by giving *Platinum* and *Origanum* to dogs, and *Platinum* and *Murex* to bitches. *Platinum* is given in either case, in high potency, a dose of 200 once a week. On the other days, the second remedy, i.e. *Origanum* for dogs and *Murex* for bitches, is given in the *6x*, four times daily.

The world-famous homoeopathic physician Dr Pierre Schmidt of Geneva saved the bull elephants of an Indian prince by giving *Platinum 10,000* when they were threatening to become a danger to human life in their sexual overexcitement. It had been intended to have the animals killed, but first an appeal was made to Dr Schmidt, and he affected a cure.

This clearly demonstrates the general natural law on which Samuel Hahnemann, the founder of homoeopathy, based his *Similia similibus curentur* — Let likes be cured by likes — a law that applies to all living creatures, both men and animals, if they are able to produce differentiated and therefore identifiable symptoms on which the choice of a remedy can be based.

If a male is getting extremely excited by a bitch on heat — barking, yowling and moaning night and day — *Agnus castus 3x-6x* will calm him down quickly and thoroughly, or also *Gelsemium 6x*, which is likewise given three times daily for a week.

Another useful remedy is *Ustilago 12x*, five times on the first day, four times on the second, and three times daily after that, until no longer required.

Onanism (Masturbation)

Chronic prostatitis is often due to the fact that many males masturbate. The excessive demand this causes — for it tends to become a habit — leads to inflammation.

The remedy for onanism is *Staphisagria 4x* three times daily, or *Staphisagria 30* once a day.

The dog is irritable and bites, he is in a nasty mood and very sensitive to touch in the hindquarter. Another characteristic is that he is extremely sensitive and easily offended if scolded. On the other hand he inclines to fits of rage, shows a lot of anger, and is best left alone in the mornings.

If there are spasms with the masturbation, *Bufo rana 15x*, twice daily, will be of help.

Reluctance to Serve

Reluctant males are made strong and capable with *Damiana 1x* and *Acidum phosphoricum 6x*.

Three doses of each are given daily, always on an empty stomach in the morning and late at night, with the midday dose not given with the feed, but ideally half an hour beforehand.

If it is suspected that the sperm is infertile, yet the dog's services appear to be indispensable, *Acidum phosphoricum 30x* may be given once a day for about three weeks.

7. Female Sex Organs

Obstetrics

Preparation

Homoeopathy has some excellent remedies to prepare for normal parturition. They are given during the second half of the pregnancy period, from the sixth week onwards.

The most important remedy is *Pulsatilla 6x*, once a day. This will prevent the possibility of abnormal presentation and of uterine inertia, ensuring a normal birth process. Complications or the need to perform a caesarian section are practically unknown with this treatment.

Diet is important prior to whelping: raw meat, rice, cereal products, vegetables, fresh fruit or uncooked green leaf vegetables, lettuce or parsley, grated carrots.

During the last two days before parturition — usually on the sixty-third day — the bitch is given a liquid diet consisting of soups or gruels, with honey or glucose added, to prevent constipation and also avoid any strain on the digestive system.

Other preparations will of course have been made earlier, such as a mild worm cure to rid the bitch of ascarids in the first half of her pregnancy, and getting her used to her whelping box, an essential item to which the mother-to-be should be introduced two weeks prior to the event, indicating it to her as her bed.

The room where the event is to take place should not be too hot (15-18°C/59-64°F). Afterwards, the wet, soiled base is best removed, replacing it with some sheeting or a blanket (definitely not an eiderdown or mattress).

If abortion should threaten during the period preceding parturition, and this may be due to a knock, a fall, bruising or an accident, *Arnica 3x* is given, 10 drops every 30 minutes, until one is sure the danger is over. *Sabina 6x* has a similar action.

If parturition has been difficult on previous occasions, a dose of *Caulophyllum 30x* is given by injection or by mouth the day before the expected event. *Caulophyllum* is particularly good for the primipara who has had a difficult time or a caesarean the first time.

After these preparations, parturition usually proceeds normally, requiring no special assistance and presenting no risk to the bitch. The remedies listed below are indeed only given if abnormalities are definitely diagnosed. They should never be given prophylactically, for they are only effective in correcting an existing disorder. If there is no problem, one allows parturition to proceed in the natural way.

If the whelps are produced at rather long intervals and there is no recognizable impediment to their appearance, parturition and normal contractions may be activated by giving *Cimicifuga 6x* at half-hourly intervals.

Uterine Inertia

The contractions really get the birth process going. If no foetus has appeared two or three hours after the onset of labour pains and the bitch is showing signs of exhaustion, it is advisable to consult a veterinary surgeon, as the situation may be dangerous.

If contractions cease when the bitch has initially been pushing, it is necessary to get good contractions going again. This is done by giving:

> *Caulophyllum 6x* and
> *Secale cornutum 6x,* every fifteen minutes in alteration.

If there are no obstacles to expulsion that would require veterinary intervention, these remedies will be successful.

When it is all over, the bitch will need *Arnica 6x* or *Bellis perennis 6x* four times daily for a few days, to prevent exhaustion and help restore the stretched birth canal to normal, until the lochia have ceased. It is a delightful sight to see a bitch with her puppies suckling contentedly as she watches over them carefully, enveloping them in maternal warmth. When each has found its nipple and the milk is flowing, all's right with the world for them.

But what if the breasts are greatly engorged, so full that the milk will not flow and it is impossible for the pups to suckle?
No need to wait until mother and pups begin to whine in unison — a few doses of *Bryonia 6x* given every two hours will release the tension and the milk line will be open for the whelps.

Agalactia (No Milk)

If milk production does not get going, a single dose of *Urtica urens 30* will stimulate it. (If there is reason later to limit it, *Urtica urens 1x* every six hours will be required.)

If there is not enough milk and artificial feeds have to be given, a mother's milk substitute is chosen that is available in powder form, needing only to be dissolved. Should this not be available, the following well-proven formula may be used for the first three weeks:

$\frac{1}{4}$ litre of whole milk at 38°C/100°F

$\frac{1}{8}$ litre of weak chamomile tea

3 or 4 tablespoonsful cream

a pinch of lime

2 drops of Vigantol

a sugar cube.

We use a graduated bottle, from the chemist's, and take great care to see that the hole in the teat is so small that the pups have to suck really hard. If the hole is too large, too much milk at once gets into the mouth to be adequately mixed with saliva, resulting in gastrointestinal problems.

During the first few days, the bottle should be offered once an hour, later every two or three hours, also at night. Attention must also be paid to quantity, for the small stomach should not be overloaded (5—10g).

The stools of the newborn are yellow and mushy, and it is important to know that the bitch triggers the excretory reflex by licking the anus. The pup needs to be cared for in this respect, too: the anus has to be massaged in a circular motion with an oiled finger, until elimination has occurred. The chamomile tea may be omitted after the first five days, and from the third or fourth week onwards cereal products are added and the pups are introduced to their food bowl.

Excess Lactation

If the pups for some reason do not require all the available milk and it is still freely flowing when they have had enough, *Urtica urens 6x*, given serveral times daily, will stop milk production.

Eclampsia

A complication which may occur in suckling bitches is parturient eclampsia. Fits or convulsions develop, with no loss of consciousness. This happens during or after parturition, but mostly for up to five weeks afterwards.

There is a sudden temperature and muscular spasms develop, with the limbs held rigidly apart.

The head is drawn back spasmodically, as though pulled by invisible forces. Finally the bitch lies on her side, breathing so fast and panting so loudly as she does so that she can be heard from a long way off.

If the eclampsia occurs in a case of pseudopregnancy, which may also happen, the symptoms are less marked.

Veterinary surgeons can effectively treat the condition with *Calcium* injections and sedatives. *Ferrum phosphoricum 6x* injected into the peritoneal cavity or into a vein has also proved effective, with the same remedy *(Ferrum phosphoricum 6x)* given every fifteen or thirty minutes by mouth.

If this form of treatment is not possible, *Hyoscyamus 30c* may be given, every ten minutes.

Recurrences are prevented with *Calcarea phosphorica 6x* and *China 6x*, six times daily in alternation for some days.

Mastitis (Inflammation of the Udder)

Mastitis is a serious condition in a bitch who has whelps to feed. It may however also develop in bitches who are not suckling, through accidents, knocks, bruising, or infection of the lactiferous ducts. All the signs of inflammation will be noted: redness, swelling, pain, a raised body temperature and apathy.

Belladonna 4x or *6x* is given initially, once an hour. It usually serves very well, but if it does not entirely deal with the situation, *Apix 3x* is also given, in alternation, particularly if the swelling is oedematous.

It can happen that the whole process is noted only when the inflammation has already progressed, with the result that the affected gland is very hard, painful and reddened. At this stage, *Bryonia 6x*, every two hours, is the remedy. It may also be the case that an abscess is already forming. Looking at the chapter on abscesses (9.6), one will then prescribe *Hepar sulphuris 3x* or *Myristica sebifera 3x*, justly famed as the 'homoeopathic knife', every two hours. This will get the abscess to point and discharge painlessly.

Calendula compresses (one teaspoon to a glass of boiled water, as usual) should be applied as often as possible. If *Calendula* or *Arnica* tincture is not available, olive oil, sunflower oil or alcohol may be used instead.

Silicea 12x is then given two or three times daily for a few days, to complete the healing process.

If there is a suspicion that the induration (hardening) is in fact a tumour, *Conium 6x* must be given three times daily, until the tumour has dissolved. This remedy may also be alternated with *Thuja 6x* or *Calcarea iodata 6x*.

Pseudopregnancy

Hormonal imbalance may also lead to pseudopregnancy. This is a condition many bitches are subject to eight or nine weeks after being on heat, i.e. at the time when they would be giving birth if they had been mated.

Pseudopregnancy may occur irrespective of whether the bitch has had pups before or not. The changes in character are quite striking: she becomes restless and hysterical, goes into hiding, builds a nest, and has an irresistible mothering instinct, treating dolls or shoes as though they were her offspring. The milk produced from her teats is the same as that produced after a normal pregnancy.

The best form of treatment would be to give her some whelps to suckle, using her as a wet nurse. Opportunities for this are rare, however, and one therefore has to use medical treatment to correct the hormonal imbalance.

Pulsatilla 30 is given three times daily for seven days, after which it will be found that the symptoms have been gently and safely cleared.

If the bitch shows marked thirst, *Cyclamen 30x* is given instead, but such cases are uncommon.

Externally, vinegar compresses (one cup of vinegar to a litre of cold water) may be applied to support the internal treatment. The object of motherly affection needs to be removed immediately, distracting the animal by taking her for long walks.

For obese lady dogs, the disease provides a unique opportunity for getting a slender waistline again, as most of them are off their feed during this period. If they do not fast of their own accord, it is important to keep the diet very scant.

There are less common cases where the restlessness occurs at night, and hardly anything will be seen of lactation. These bitches require *Lilium tigrinum 6x* or *30x*, every four hours.

Asafoetida 4x is another useful remedy, given when irritable, nervous restlessness predominates. If hysteria is marked, *Ignatia 6x* should be given (see under Constitutional Types, Chapter 17).

Compared to hormone therapy, the above methods will result in the pseudopregnancies growing milder and less marked each time. Later on they will be hardly noticeable, only rarely requiring treatment.

French practitioners recommend a weekly dose of *Ignatia 200x* as an alternative to be given after the bitch has been on heat, to prevent pseudopregnancy.

Infertility

Infertility is becoming more and more of a problem for many breeders and animal lovers. The cause may be endocrine failure. A diet consisting entirely of preserved foods is another suspected cause, but exact data are not yet available. Experience has shown, however, that feeding all the animals in a breeding establishment on deep frozen meat can be responsible for protracted oestrus and infertility of bitches.

A missing oestrus is stimulated with:

   Aristolochia 3x and
   Cimicifuga 6x

10 drops of each twice daily, given three weeks before oestrus is due to occur, basing one's calculations on the fact that bitches come on heat twice a year. Veterinary surgeons also have an injection preparation available that among other things contains *Aristolochia clematitis*. The injections have to be given with an interval of two weeks between them.

Bitches who do go on heat but refuse mating, biting the male, during the fertile period from the eleventh to the fourteenth day, need *Sepia 6x*, three times daily, for three weeks beforehand.

As a general treatment for infertility, *Aristolochia 3x* and *Sepia 6x* may be given, alternating day by day, particularly if the bitch has been known to drive away the male on earlier occasions.

Another method of triggering oestrus is to give *Pulsatilla 30* three times daily for a week.

Having given the system this intensive treatment with a relatively high potency, one waits to see how it responds. It is advisable to repeat four weeks later, in case the first treatment did not match the cycle — and considering the irregularity of oestrus this is certainly possible.

Pyometra (Uterine Infection)

A justifiably dreaded condition seen in older bitches is metritis, inflammation of the uterus. It oftens occurs after oestrus, but may also develop weeks later. Any febrile condition during this period may develop into pyometra.

The symptoms are a more or less marked failure to thrive and a discharge from the vagina, sometimes only slight, that serves as a definite indication that pus has collected in the uterus. Such a discharge is certainly no indication for total hysterectomy, which is invariably followed by obesity.

The form of metritis known as pyometra provides an excellent illustration of the valuable service homoeopathy is able to render. Hourly doses of *Pulsatilla 4x* or *6x* will cause a 'fountain' to flow that will cleanse the uterus from the considerable volume of secretions it contains and bring about a cure. *Lachesis, Pyrogenium* and *Echinacea angustifolia* given in addition will deal with the dangerous infection.

French practitioners treat the condition with the triad:

> *Sepia 6x*
> *Helonias dioica 6x*
> *Hydrastis 6x*

in equal parts, three or four times daily, complementing this with a teaspoonful of *Kalium iodatum 3x* in 100g of water after every meal, as this has a profound action on the mucosa.

We have also seen good results with *Sabina 8x*, not so much in the acute, but in subacute and chronic forms. *Sabina* may also be used as follow-up therapy.

Sequelae of Sterilization

When the ovaries have been removed in a total hysterectomy and after sterilization, bitches frequently show hormonal imbalance leading to obesity or to stones and gravel in the bladder.

In younger animals, *Aristolochia clematitis 3x* will normalize the situation to some extent. *Thuja 3x* should be given in addition, administering both remedies two or three times daily for some weeks. Older animals will usually respond to *Thuja 8x* on its own. *Calcarea carbonica 4x* or *6x* may be prescribed in addition.

It is always a difficult situation to deal with, for the animals grow indolent once the ovaries or testes have been removed. Even lots of exercise will not be enough to stimulate metabolism sufficiently in the long run.

Regulation of Hormonal Imbalance (Oestrus)

Both the timing and the degree of oestrus are regulated by the following combination:

> *Aristolochia clematitis 3x*

Pulsatilla 3x

Apis mellifica 3x

in equal parts, ten drops three times daily for three weeks and after that for ten days in the month, until oestrus becomes entirely normal, i.e. occurs twice a year, and bleeding does not continue for more than ten days, with the fertile period of eleven days then following.

Some Special Hints:

If a bitch on heat is biting to keep the male off after the bleeding phase, i.e. at the time when she should admit him, this is an indication for *Sepia*.

If the bitch will not accept her pups, or does not care for them, and indeed eats them, this is an indication for *Sepia* (*Sepia 6x* or *12x*, or a single dose of *Sepia 200c*).

The deplorable habit of holding on to an unwilling bitch during the act, forcing it on her, is another indication for *Sepia* in so far as the remedy, given for some time beforehand, will make such rape unnecessary. Birth complications are not uncommon when mating has been forced.

8. Urinary Tract

Cystitis (Inflammation of the Bladder)

There are many possible causes for cystitis. Getting wet, or thoroughly chilled for some time, with movement restricted so that the dog is unable to keep his circulation going properly, can easily lead to it. The homoeopathic remedy for chills, *Dulcamara 6x*, is indicated, first every half hour, and then at longer intervals as the condition improves.

Blood in the urine after an accident, after being struck in the abdomen or after a fight, is an early indication of bladder injury. If vascular damage is minimal, *Hamamelis 2x* given for a short time will soon deal with this. If the injury is more severe, and particularly if the general condition is not good, surgery will be urgently required.

If a well-trained dog is forced, due to carelessness, to hold on to his urine for some time, the bladder may become overextended. In chronic cases this will lead to strangury (constant desire to urinate linked with pain). The dog no longer has control where the passing of his water is concerned, and a house-trained animal is no longer clean. *Petroselinum 6x* will bring rapid relief in these cases, as it does in enuretic children.

Much more serious is the severe cystitis caused by bacteria gaining entrance from the kidneys or the bloodstream. The first sign will be a reduction in the general state of health; urination is irregular, the urine is cloudy and may also contain blood.

Echinacea angustifolia mother tincture and *Terebinthina 3x*, once an hour in alternation, will be required, with *Hamamelis 2x* added if the urine contains blood.

If there is strangury with the cystitis and only a few drops of blood are produced, *Cantharis 5x* is an outstanding remedy. In very acute cases it may be given every fifteen minutes, otherwise at two-hourly intervals.

minutes, otherwise at two-hourly intervals.

The patient will of course be given a mild herb tea with special action on the kidneys and bladder, sweetened with honey if desired, and will be protected from cold and exertion.

The prescription for occasional haemorrhage from the bladder due to gravel, with blood in the urine at intervals is:

Terebinthina 3x
Berberis 3x

each given three times daily.

If the bleeding does not respond, badly infected molars may be the cause.

Paralysis of the Bladder

Nervous disorders of various origin may lead to two forms of paralysis.

The first results in retention of urine, whilst with the second, the dog is unable to retain his urine. He is 'dribbling', losing small amounts inadvertently.

Urinary retention is no doubt the lesser of the two evils. The bladder will be distended, and may extend to the nearest ribs, but mechanical pressure with both hands, first overcoming a certain resistance, will soon cause it to empty, unless the blockage is due to gravel. If pressure does not succeed, *Petroselinum 1x-3x* given every fifteen minutes will help, or else a catheter.

Paralysis of the sphincter, causing constant 'dribbling', is treated with *Hyoscyamus 6x*.

If a nervous bladder is in evidence only at night, causing a well-trained dog to pass water without even noticing it, *Petroselinum 6x* will again be the remedy, as for children who wet the bed during their first sleep. Older dogs are better given *Causticum 6x*.

If the paralysis is due to spinal disease, *Strychninum nitricum 12x* will be required, three times daily.

If the paralysis occurs as a sequel to an accident, *Arnica 4x-30x* needs to be given, depending on the amount of time which has passed since the accident. The *4x* three times daily if it is a matter of days, the *30x* once a day if it was months ago.

If the paralysis is due to cerebral involvement in a case of distemper, *Gelsemium 12x* or *15x* is given twice daily. The same remedy, *Gelsemium*, in the *6x* is often effective in dealing with the 'tears of joy' young dogs are apt to shed, those well-known types who tend to pass water with every emotion, be it joy or fear — not exactly a pleasure for the mistress of the house.

Stones and Gravel in the Bladder

Urinary calculi will cause variable degrees of trouble when passing water. They have as much of a detrimental effect on the general health as kidney stones do, though the latter are much less common.

Small calculi the size of grains of sand (gravel) will be passed in the urine without causing the dog much trouble or being much noticed by the person looking after the dog. However, when gravel or small stones obstruct the urethra, *Cantharis 5x* will bring instant relief for a bitch. In dogs, surgical intervention will become inevitable, as mechanical obstruction to the flow of urine is a dangerous condition that may become fatal as the system becomes poisoned with toxins from the retained urine. Whether conservative treatment is still possible or surgery has to be resorted to, it will always be necessary also to deal with the underlying cause.

We give:

Lycopodium 30x, once a day for a week, and
Berberis 3x, three times daily for two weeks.

When the salts have already crystallized and stones have been formed, these may be as big as the bladder itself. Such solitary calculi must be surgically removed, followed by homoeopathic treatment to prevent the development of new calculi. In other words, it is necessary to deal with the metabolic disorder which has caused the salts to crystallize.

The constitutional remedy must be found (see Chapter 17). If this is not possible, the following, well-proven remedies are given, adhering strictly to the sequence shown:

Sulphur 12x
Calcarea carbonica 12x
Lycopodium 12x

Each is given three times daily on its own, for two weeks. The whole course of alterative therapy therefore takes six weeks.

Attention must also be paid to diet. The easiest from the owner's point of view is a ready-made diet food designed to relieve the strain on the kidneys. This is obtainable from veterinary surgeons and should be given for some weeks.

Another method, equally good, is to use the following diet:

As little as possible of protein from dead animals, i.e. meat, with preference given to protein products from living animals - milk, soft cheese, eggs. It is safe to add vegetables, rice, potatoes, a little boiled fish, and occasionally a few dog biscuits.

Stones in the gall bladder or in the spleen, very occasionally found if the dog is X-rayed for some other reason, are treated with *Calculi biliarii 8x*, three times daily.

Nephritis (Inflammation of the Kidneys)

Acute nephritis is caused by different organisms (distemper, Stuttgart disease) or bacterial toxins reaching the kidneys via the bloodstream (foci of infection near the teeth, in the tonsils or uterus). Chemical poisons may also be responsible (tar, mercury, salicylates), or unsuitable items in the diet (seasoning mixes, salt, pepper, salami). A common cold or an ascending inflammation of the bladder are other possible causes of nephritis.

Sudden onset, with shivering and trembling, tiredness and apathy as well as loss of appetite are the early signs. The dog walks stiffly and with difficulty, his back arched, and is highly sensitive to pressure in the kidney region. Vomiting and diarrhoea may also occur. The quantity of urine passed is greatly reduced, the urine is cloudy, dark, and often contains blood.

This acute stage, when the dog is drinking no more than usual or nothing at all, is treated with:

Apis 3x and

Cantharis 5x

every thirty minutes in alternation, and less frequently as the condition improves. This is followed with *Berberis 3x*, three times daily until recovery is complete.

If blood is passed, *Hamamelis 2x*, or *Millefolium 3x* may be given in addition.

As to diet, the strain on the kidneys is relieved by giving neither food nor drink for the first two days. After that, easily digestible foods such as milk, rice, gruel, only very small quantities of meat, eggs, and tea with honey are given.

Chronic nephritis develops very insidiously. There is no pain, so that it tends to go undiscovered for a long time, despite the offensive uraemic smell from the mouth.

It is only when the condition has reached an advanced stage that the tormenting thirst develops which drives the dog to drink from every puddle and every pool, and indeed to lick up his own urine. He will accordingly pass water frequently at night. A poor appetite leading to loss of weight, digestive disorders, eczema and hair loss are further stages on the road to cirrhosis of the kidney.

Apart from a diet designed to relieve the kidney, one will of course try to stop the process, or at least slow it down.

Experience has shown the following to be most effective:

Mercurius solubilis 12x, three times daily until the animal feels well and the thirst is bearable.

If there is massive albuminuria (presence of albumin in the urine), the heartbeats are irregular, and symptoms appear in the eye (keratitis), *Serum anguillae 6x* is given.

Severe cases, with a tendency to weakness, great emaciation and oedema, when the patient takes frequent small drinks and often vomits the liquid he has taken, with restlessness at night, aggravation between 1 and 3 a.m., and a great desire for warmth, require *Arsenicum album 6x*, three times daily.

In nephrosis with greatly elevated residual nitrogen levels in the blood, *Lespedeza Sieboldi 1x* or *Lespenephryl* ® [1] may be tried.

There are limits to what treatment can achieve in these cases. If the condition is advanced and the dog uraemic, all attempts at treatment should be abandoned, unless there is a very real chance of restoring health.

It should also be mentioned that resistant and persistent nephritis in younger animals, when there is no appreciable sign of a response and in spite of everything the outcome is (often) fatal, may also be due to toxoplasmosis. Another condition to be considered with chronic kidney disease is an occult Stuttgart disease (leptospirosis). Blood tests will lead to the identification of these two diseases.

---

[1]Pharmaceutical preparation containing an extract of Lespedeza capitata (Endopharm) — Translator.

9. Skin Complaints

Hair Loss

Except for the times when the coat is shed in spring and autumn, hair loss is always indicative of metabolic disorder, the cause of which must be ascertained.

If there are scales as well as hair loss, particularly in the lumbar and sacral region, *Sulphur 6x* is given for some time, three times daily.

Natrum muriaticum 12x, three times daily for at least three weeks, is the remedy for animals who are fed largely on convenience foods, with the result that hair loss persists throughout the year.

In this condition, the hair comes away as soon as one takes hold of it (added to which the dog is thirsty, bites suddenly, is easily moved to anger, and also tires easily).

When circumscribed bald patches appear symmetrically in the lumbar region or on the back of older bitches, *Sepia 6x* will in most cases correct the hormonal imbalance (comparable to the change of life in humans).

Obese dogs who are also lazy, depressed, chilly, nervous and constipated and are not very keen on walking (hypothyroidism), whose skin is dry and cracked, with rhagades (fissures) around orifices (e.g. at the transition from skin to mucosa), will do extremely well on *Graphites 8x*, which will cure the hair loss (1 tablet three times daily).

If there is no particular indication for any specific treatment, *Thallium aceticum 12x* may be tried, 1 tablet twice daily for three weeks or longer.

An occasional dose of *Sulphur 30* given to dogs whose coat has gone dull will greatly stimulate metabolism, so that the coat regains its lustre. At the same time, live yeast, baker's yeast, may be given as a food supplement, adding a piece the size of a cherry to the rations three or four times a week. This effectively changes the intestinal flora (at low cost), a measure that by a long roundabout route which we need not go into, also benefits hair growth.

It is self-evident and quite natural that overheated rooms and dry air will also cause hair loss. In that case, a change of location to fresh air and cool surroundings will be all that is required.

Hair loss after serious illness	*China 6x*
	Ferrum metallicum 5x
Hair loss between the shoulder blades, hair breaking	*Lycopodium 12x*, also massage with salicyl alcohol
Hair loss, especially from underbelly	*Silicea 6x-12x*
Loss of beard hairs	*Kalium phosphoricum 6x*
Hair loss after giving birth	*Sepia 12x*

Matting of Hair

Matting of hair, also known as trichoma, particularly behind the ears and on the extremities, is generally an indication for *Sulphur*.

Sulphur 6x is given three times daily for some time, after removal of the matted hair or shearing the dog.

Acidum fluoricum 15x and *Psorinum 10x*, depending on the type, are also useful remedies after *Sulphur*.

Hair Breaking

The breaking of hair usually starts on the back, between the shoulder blades, and may spread to the rest of the body. It is a condition fairly commonly seen in long-haired breeds such as Sheepdogs and Chows.

The underlying cause is always a liver condition, though this is generally still subclinical and not demonstrable in laboratory tests. The dogs show greater or lesser variation in appetite, appearing to be hungry, yet not wanting any more after a few mouthfuls. *Lycopodium* will rapidly and safely correct the liver problem.

People who look after dogs professionally and therefore have little time, are advised to give one tablet of *Lycopodium 30x* at night, otherwise the treatment is *Lycopodium 12x* three times daily.

Lycopodium in the 18th *LM* potency, 5 drops twice daily, is the remedy if the breaking of hair has become chronic.

As soon as the blockage in the liver has been cleared, normal hair growth will start again. This is also why we do not consider external treatment necessary.

Dandruff

Quite often a dog will appear bright and lively, yet suffers from complete dryness of skin, with enormous quantities of dandruff. This is noted particularly when grooming, most of all in the sacral region.

Sulphur 6x is an excellent remedy if given three times daily for some time. It will however also be necessary to make a change in diet, reducing the amount of convenience foods or, even better, omitting them altogether. If care is also taken to see that the dog gets plenty of fresh air and exercise, his condition will improve rapidly, and he will have a healthy, shining coat.

A typical indication for *Sulphur* is a strong 'smell of dog'.

When the scales come off in large flakes, particularly in old dogs, *Arsenicum album 6x* will be required.

Another way of finding the right remedy is this:

skin red, warm or even hot	*Sulphur*
skin pale or cool	*Arsenicum album.*

Allergy (Urticaria or Nettlerash)

Sudden chills, external irritants and the toxic effects of certain metabolic products arising from digestive disorders may on occasion trigger an allergy in short-haired breeds, particularly Boxers, Dachshunds, Dobermans and Dalmatians.

Lumps and swellings will appear in seconds all over the coat, or sometimes only in circumscribed areas. The dog looks as if he had been stung all over by bees. The head gets swollen, and frequently there is skin irritation. Puppies are particularly prone to it during second dentition.

The attacks will pass off quickly after a few doses of *Apis 3x* which in view of the rapid development of the condition is first given every ten or twenty minutes, and less frequently as the condition improves. If a higher potency of *Apis*, say the 30th, is available, this may also be given, but not more than a few doses.

Cold compresses with vinegar water also give relief. A cupful of ordinary vinegar is added to a litre of cold water. For the next few days, the dog is kept on a scant diet, with a pinch of Carlsbad Salt or kaolin added to the rations.

If a dog is prone to urticaria, with the condition recurring at intervals, *Apis* is again used to deal with the acute phase, and this is then followed with *Calcarea carbonica 12x*, 1 tablet three times daily for three weeks.

Autohaemotherapy has also proved effective in chronic cases. For this, one drop of blood is mixed with 100 drops of 35 per cent alcohol in a vial and potentized by the homoeopathic method to *5c, 6c* and *7c*.

The patient is then given first the *5c*, five drops twice daily, then the *6c*, ten drops once a day, and finally the *7c*, ten drops once a week, always at night, if possible, before going to bed.

This form of treatment, using the potentized blood of the patient, has given outstanding results in humans and also in dogs (and cats) when employed to treat allergic conditions, furunculosis (recurrent boils), tonsillitis, coryza, otitis and bronchitis.

Veterinary surgeons with experience in homoeopathy will use this method when indicated, making up the medication themselves.

Pruritus (Skin Irritation) and Mange

Pruritus

If there is pruritus, the first step is to look for parasites: fleas (especially at the base of the ear, in the croup and on the underbelly), sucking lice (in the margins of the ears), biting lice and harvest mites in late summer (usually between the toes and in the underbelly).

A single flea will be enough nowadays to set a dog scratching and biting.

If in doubt, therefore, always straight into the bathtub. A bath with an antiparasitic preparation added to the water is preferable to sprays and powders, for it gets right through to the skin instead of reaching only the outer coat.

Pruritus is always only a symptom of some disease, and a veterinary surgeon must be consulted to determine the cause. The possible causes are so numerous that clearly there cannot be just a single remedy to treat the condition.

Dry skin irritation with scales, redness of the skin and a desire for coolness calls for *Sulphur 6x*, four times daily. If high *Sulphur* potencies are available, e.g. the *200*, a single dose of this is given once a week.

If the skin is dry and the dog wants warmth, *Arsenicum album 6x* should be considered, particularly if there is night-time aggravation starting just before midnight and the dog is exhausted by this.

If a bitch suffers from skin irritation at night, and there are also red patches, the cause is probably hormonal and the condition will respond to *Pulsatilla 200* given morning and night for three days.

Severe pruritus at all stages of inflammatory skin changes such as pustules, eczema, blisters, ulcers, inflammation of the hypodermis with a tendency to gangrene requires *Kreosotum 4x*, one tablet six, five and four times daily. All secretions are offensive and cause soreness of the skin and mucosa.

Mange

This troublesome condition, passed on from dog to dog, is not often seen nowadays. It is caused by a mite.

In adult dogs it starts on the head, which is also why it is sometimes known as head mange. It then spreads to the forehead, ears and eyes, moving down to the neck, paws and trunk. Folds develop in the skin with irritation worse from warmth, and a bran-like material that has an unpleasant smell of mice covers the affected areas.

In younger animals, mange develops first on the neck and belly.

Animals suffering from mange must be isolated if at all possible, particularly if there are other animals in the house. Beds and bedding, brushes, combs and collars need to be carefully disinfected to prevent recurrence.

The condition is treated with a preparation recommended by the veterinary surgeon, usually a bath product requiring repeated treatments, or a liniment. Additional methods are best discussed with a veterinary surgeon, as the risk of contagion may present a number of problems.

Homoeopathy can only help indirectly, by alteration and strengthening of the skin environment.

Sulphur, given three times daily, will initiate the process.

Eczema

Eczema is a non-infectious skin condition using the body as a safety valve to eliminate metabolic toxins. The body, as it were, has a rubbish-disposal problem. Therefore it is not a good idea to block such eruptions with ointments or by painting on fluids. They will only reappear elsewhere and sooner or later give rise to further disease.

Moist or weeping eczema consists essentially in a serous discharge from various skin areas. The dog will lick, bite and scratch, opening up the sore places. The skin areas may be as large as the palm of a hand and may become infected through the biting and scratching. Dry eczema on the other hand means that the skin remains dry, and irritation is much less serious.

Eczema may be due to a variety of causes: lack of a balanced diet, too much tinned food, dogs having a sensitive skin from birth, and also disorders of the excretory system (liver and kidneys), in the intestine or a hormonal imbalance. Lack of fresh air and exercise generally plays a major role.

What can be done about it? It is always advisable to make a change in the diet, even if the dog does not like it and refuses to accept the new diet for some days. If he has had too much tinned food before, fresh meat should now be given. A dog who had had too much meat should now be given more cereal products and fish.

The cleansing treatment described earlier (page 00) will help in every case of acute eczema. It is one hundred per cent effective, making all injections and other medical treatment unnecessary, providing it is followed exactly. If it is felt undesirable to make the dog fast in this condition, exactly the right homoeopathic remedy must be found to treat him.

There are three basic remedies to be considered in any case of eczema:

Sulphur

The remedy for autointoxication. The signs are hot skin, with itching eruptions, and redness of orifices such as eyes, mouth, ears, prepuce, vagina, and anal mucosa.

Sulphur is used for dry eruptions that itch and are covered with scales. The *Sulphur* patient has an offensive, unhealthy smell. The *6x* is given every three hours in acute cases, the *12x* three times daily for chronic eczema. It is not advisable to go higher than the *6x* in acute cases.

Psorinum

The patient has marked sensitivity to cold, an unpleasant body-odour, and moist eruptions.

The skin eruption is frequently linked with a purulent, brown, foetid, stinking discharge from the ear. Pruritus is very marked indeed.

A daily dose of *Psorinum* will be an effective basic treatment in these cases.

If the distinction between dry and moist is not adequate, special local features are considered, to differentiate the following remedies:

Eczema in joint flexures and on the inner aspects of extremities calls for *Natrum muriaticum 12x*, three times daily. Eczema in the anal region: *Paeonia 3x*. Eczema of the scrotum: *Rhus toxicodendron 30*, once a day; *Croton 6x*, four times daily. Eczema of the female genitalia: *Rhus toxicodenron 30*, once a day, and *Mercurius solubilis 6x*, three times daily. Eczema between the toes: *Silicea 12x*. Eczema on the soles, eczemata that are worse in winter: *Petroleum 12x*. Summer eczema: *Acidum fluoricum 6x, and Kreosotum 4x*.

Chronic dry eczema with scaly eruptions (like bran) that bleed when scratched but do not weep, also pruritus at night (between 1 and 3 a.m.) and excoriating discharge from the ear, with the patient usually skinny: *Arsenicum album 6x*.

Natrum muriaticum

A weeping eczema of the type described for *Natrum muriaticum* has become more common in recent years, when the consumption of commercial dog foods has been increasing. *Natrum muriaticum* is a remedy often quoted by those who like to question the value of homoeopathy. Can one really expect a useful medicinal action from common salt, considering the quantities of it normally ingested, and the fact that it is given in very small doses?

Yet if the right diagnosis has been made, common salt, prepared and prescribed on homoeopathic principles, is a miracle drug, for the simple reason that is normalizes disorders of salt metabolism. Physiological saline surrounds every cell in the body.

Commercial dog foods are known to contain additives that often have an effect on this metabolism. A healthy organism will eliminate these via the skin, through eczema.

What is the appearance of a *Natrum muriaticum* eruption?

It may be noted in pups if after being taken from their mother they were given a commercial food in the pet shop, until sold. They do not like being touched, their skin being painfully sensitive all over. They are extremely nervous, suffer from hair loss and eczema in the axilla and in the joint flexures, and sometimes also fissures in the anus or in the nose. The animals are also easily tired and extremely chilly. It is unbelievable how quickly such a sad little bundle will recover after treatment with *Natrum muriaticum 12x*, three times daily.

If there is fungal infection (mycosis) as well as eczema, we give *Cinnabaris 6x* several times daily in addition. *Acidum formicicum 15x*, twice daily, has also proved effective in such cases. Finally we add a tablet of *Berberis 4x* to each dose, as a drainage remedy that will help to eliminate toxins.

Dry eczemas are connected with a functional disorder of the liver. Moist eczemas on the other hand indicate malfunction of the kidney, even when laboratory tests do not yet confirm this.

Mercurius solubilis 200 is the remedy of choice for this. It is given three times daily, as far as possible at eight-hourly intervals (early in the morning, on an empty stomach, then at midday, and late at night), but not for more than five days. *Mercurius solubilis* will prove effective in the majority of cases, saving the trouble of external measures such as shearing, applying ointments, baths etc.

The highly acute type of weeping eczema frequently seen in Chows during the summer should be treated with four doses of *Mercurius solubilis 200* (six-hourly, including at night) on each of the first two days, and then three times daily on the third to fifth day. Sometimes, if the moist eczema involves severe pruritus and offensive secretions, *Cantharis 5x* every two hours may be the remedy, or, if there is reddening and vesicles are forming, *Rhus toxicodendron 12x*, and if vesicles and whitish crusts with yellow pus are noted, *Mezereum 4x*.

Some types of eczema have honey yellow secretions, found mainly in the ear passages and external ear, around the eyes, on the lips, in the joint flexures or on the genitalia. In these cases one will think of *Graphites 4x*, three times daily. It is a good idea to give *Berberis 4x*, also three times daily, in addition, as a drainage remedy.

Treatment may be supported locally, to reduce the itching, with fluids such as *honey water* (*hydromel*), *Hypericum oil*, *Calendula* ointment or compresses, or *Calendula* tincture applied with a dropper directly to the open lesions, several times a day.

For dry eczema, ordinary potato flour or cornflour may be used as a dusting powder.

Itching eczemas with hair loss in older dogs that are due to hormonal imbalance, respond well to *Aristolochia clematitis 2x*, in both dogs and bitches. If the eczema has a strikingly unpleasant smell, the 'pong remedy' *Kreosotum 4x* may also be considered.

Furunculosis (Boils), Acne

Funculosis affects the dorsum of the nose or the lower jaw in dogs. If it does not respond to *Hepar sulphuris 6x* three times daily within ten days, the following combination should be given:

> *Aristolochia clematitis 15x*
> *Mezereum 4x*
> *Rhus toxicodendron 4x*

a dose of each three times daily. These remedies may also be given together.

Acne of old dogs, particularly on the jaw, requires *Kalium bromatum 12x*.

Callouses on the elbows or knees will respond to:

> *Graphites 4x* and

Antimonium crudem 15x

four times daily in alternation, and at night a tablet of:

Calcarea fluorata 30x,

for two or three weeks.

Abscesses

Abscesses are an infectious condition with all the signs of inflammation: redness, heat, pain, swelling and pus formation.

Hepar sulphuris 3x, every two hours, assists pus formation, allowing the abscess to come to a head, until it opens spontaneously.

If spontaneous discharge of pus is delayed, the 'homoeopathic knife', *Myristica sebifera 3x,* 5 drops several times daily, will prove highly effective. It will only rarely be necessary to open the abscess with a scalpel. Useful external applications are warm linseed or mashed baked potato compresses (potatoes in a bag, not too hot — it is best to test the temperature against the back of one's hand). Compresses or bathing with *Calendula* or *Echinacea* tincture are always helpful (1 teaspoonful or 25 drops to a glass of boiled water).

Silicea 12x, 1 tablet twice daily, will make sure that there are no residual scars. This remedy needs to be given once the abscess has opened.

Cold abscesses, with little evidence of inflammation, are uncommon. They occur in cases of tuberculosis and are treated with *Mercurius solubilis 6x* or *Hepar sulphuris 6x.* Persistent fistulae require *Silicea 12x.*

Whitlows (paronychia), inflammation near the nail, and interdigital abscesses are also treated with *Hepar 3x,* every two hours.

Once the abscess has discharged, two or three daily doses of *Silicea 6x* for a few days are advisable, to ensure no complications arise during the healing process. In untreated cases, one often sees fistulae developing.

There is an elegant solution if an abscess is caught very early, before pus collects:

Hepar sulphuris 30, and an hour later

Pyrogenium 30, a single dose

Unfortunately this will only apply on rare occasions, as the early stage frequently goes unnoticed.

Mycosis (Fungus Infection)

Fungus infection can occur only if the skin environment has been damaged. The skin has a protective coating of lactic acid and this, together with normal sebum production, has a fungicidal action.

It is not sufficient to treat the skin locally, using measures to combat the fungus. The 'terrain' needs to be improved, restoring the abnormal metabolism and hence skin function to normal.

This can be achieved with the principal skin remedies used in homoeopathic medicine:

Sulphur
Calcarea carbonica
Lycopodium
Arsenicum album

These are constitutional remedies. Their action is general, but they also give outstanding local results.

Sulphur

The mucous membranes are red, particularly in orifices such as the mouth, anus, vagina, and frequently also the inner ear; better from cold; often constipated, or constipation and diarrhoea in one and the same stool; dandruff.

Calcarea carbonica Hahnemannii

Lymphatic type with retarded growth, head ponderous, big stomach, a great eater, greedy for fruit and eggs, likes milk but this causes diarrhoea, many gastrointestinal problems.

Lycopodium

Belly blown up some hours after taking food; liver sensitive and painful. Boils, acne, intertrigo, eczema. If without appetite, then in a very characteristic way: comes rushing up when he hears the clatter of the food bowl, apparently very hungry, sniffs at the food, takes perhaps a mouthful or two, and walks off. Great appetite, but feels full up. Better in the evenings, when he'll also take food.

Arsenicum album

Tends to be skinny and exhausted, but despite this, is restless and fearful at night, especially after midnight; carrion-like smell of excretions; scaly eruptions, like bran, bleeding when scratched but not weeping. Frequent drinks, but small quantities only.

If the patient fits one of these types, the remedy is given three times daily, using the *12x*.

If none of the four remedies are indicated, *Cinnabaris 4x-6x* may be given, 1 tablet three times daily for two or three weeks if the infection is more serious. The usual antimycotic ointments may be used externally. Ointments containing *Echinacea* are also suitable, though they only act indirectly on the fungal mycelium.

Chronic forms of mycosis that have persisted for months or even years and have not so far responded to treatment, appearing now in one site, now in another, and resisting even the most intensive, massive form of treatment, will respond well to *Psorinum* in the 18th *LM* potency, 5 drops twice daily, shaking the bottle ten times before giving it, which is something one always has to do with *LM* potencies.

Finally, if fungal infection is widespread, another good method is to change the pH of the skin. The dog is bathed or washed in a 0.5 per cent copper sulphate solution on three consecutive days (5g of copper sulphate in 10 litres of water).

Parasites

A really healthy animal will not usually be subject to parasitic infestation. The lactic acid coat protecting the skin makes life unpleasant for the parasites if it is well-developed and intact, and soon causes them to depart again.

A natural remedy that has been found to strengthen this protective coat is *Sulphur*, either in the form of *flowers of sulphur* or in a homoeopathic potency such as the *4x* or *6x*. *Sulphur* is eliminated via the skin (as the great surgeon August Bier has shown in his experiments). It changes the skin environment the same way baker's yeast does. Fleas, lice and harvest mites are destroyed by application of a commercially available antiparasitic shampoo.

Ticks have a screw-like structure on their heads. They bore into the tissues by turning anti-clockwise, and release themselves by turning clockwise. A tick can therefore be 'unscrewed' by turning it round once or twice in a clockwise direction, applying gentle traction. The head with its dreaded pincers will not tear off with this method, avoiding complications such as dermatitis or an abscess forming.

Ticks were until recently considered harmless parasites, at least in Central Europe, and it was thought they did not transmit diseases. It appears, however, that a virus has spread among ticks that will cause tick-borne encephalitis if an animal is bitten. The condition has so far been seen in Austria, Yugoslavia, Poland, Russia, Sweden, and in Germany in the Black Forest and in the Bavarian Forest. This in itself is sufficient reason to remove ticks by hand and avoid wooded areas known to be heavily infested with these parasites.

It appears that they have now also been transferred to the Odenwald region and the area around Frankfurt. There have been cases, fortunately only few, where dogs infested with ticks have shown encephalomyelitic symptoms such as sudden disorientation, stupor and apathy about one hour after the ticks were removed — which appears to be the triggering factor, as the parasites had been present in the coat for some time. The patients would stand in a corner for hours, or go into a long sleep.

On the other hand there may be states of excitement, fearfulness, spasms, running in a circle, or, if the process is one-sided, the head is held at an angle, with rolling movements of the whole body, and there is paralysis in the hind quarter.

For acute states of excitement, *Belladonna 4x,* given every fifteen to thirty minutes to begin with, is the remedy; and for paralysis, *Nux vomica 6x.* If there is a mixture of both, the two remedies are given in alternation.

Warts

Warts are epidermal tumours that may develop in any part of the body. Older animals are particularly prone to warts.

Thuja is the principal remedy. More than 50 per cent of warts will respond to it. *Thuja 30x* is given once daily for a week, and then at longer intervals.

Tincture of *Thuja* may in addition be applied externally. *Thuja* warts are fissured, cauliflower-like, they tend to itch and will bleed easily. Another excellent wart remedy for older dogs is *Calcarea carbonica 200,* for small, round, itching warts.

Warts in the ear call for *Calcarea carbonica 12x* in the mornings and *Causticum 12x* at night, to be continued until the warts have shrunk and disappeared.

Warts responding to *Causticum* are very hard, small, and occur all over the body, with a preference for the face, the eyebrows, the nose and the forefeet. The remedy is used in the same way as *Thuja.*

Warts showing a preference for the eyelids, the front paws or between the claws, are *Acidum nitricum* warts: painful, bleeding easily, soft, moist, itching. These are the warts one sees on the eyelids, causing constant lacrimation, and which keep recurring after surgical removal.

Homoeopathic treatment for warts consists in treating the metabolic disorder that has led to the development of the warts, and restoring it to normal. This will prevent recurrence, and existing warts will shrink or drop off. It does not always succeed, but it does so in many cases.

Warts that come up suddenly in large numbers in the oral cavity are a condition occasionally seen in young animals. The warts are grey in appearance, have an offensive smell, and interfere with feeding. *Acidum nitricum 6x* three times daily, and a single dose of *Calcarea carbonica* for some days, will soon get rid of this problem.

10. Nervous System

Mental States

Fear and Anxiety

Today, more than ever, our charges are subject to all kinds of stresses —
city traffic, noise, exhaust gases, their owner's nervousness, unsatis-
factory living conditions, or sometimes excessive spoiling, with the
result that anxiety symptoms develop over the course of time, unless the
dog was already born with them — symptoms that definitely call for
treatment. There are many ways in which homoepathy can also be used
to treat such mental states.

The mildest form of nervous condition is the constant barking some
dogs are prone to, a considerable nuisance to everybody. A weekly dose
of *Lachesis 200* will usually achieve a good response.

'Nervous biters' are rather unpleasant dogs to have around. They will
bite quite suddenly, with no warning growl beforehand. The type
occurs in many breeds, and their owners will no doubt find it a great
relief to be rid of the problem. *Belladonna 30x* once a day should deal
with this, concluding the treatment with a single dose of *Calcarea
carbonica 200* or *1000*.

Dogs who give advance notice of their intention to bite, by growling
or barking, always have to be kept on a lead of course, as they would
otherwise attack any other member of the breed, particularly if smaller
than themselves. These dogs require *Hyoscyamus 30x* once a day, with
the *200* or *1000* given at longer intervals as the condition improves.

Nux vomica may also be considered in such a case. In human
medicine, this is the remedy for nervous characters who flare up at the
least thing, suffer from digestive disorders and are at times subject to
anxiety. The animal world has its mirror image of this in the aggressive

dog who would like to tear any visitor to pieces and, having got used to him, still wants to attack again as he leaves. *Nux vomica 30x* is well worth trying in this case.

Dogs have forty times better hearing than we do. Thunderstorms and the bangs made by fireworks on Guy Fawkes Night are torture to many of man's friends. *Borax 3x*, 1 tablet three times daily, starting a fortnight before the event in the case of Guy Fawkes Night, will help, unless it becomes necessary to use stronger sedatives.

Patients who have found an earlier visit to the veterinary surgeon anything but a pleasure are easily inclined to turn back on the surgery doorstep when another visit is made. This kind of fear is counteracted by *Phosphorus 200* given one hour beforehand.

If an old dog who is physically fit starts to walk about at night when everybody else is asleep, restlessly making it known that he wants to go out, his owner, having complied, will be surprised to find that there was no reason for this at all. The dog will not relieve himself but soon return to the house, only to continue walking about restlessly.

A single dose of *Arsenicum album 30* or *200* will be the remedy, and the nights will be peaceful again. The dose may be repeated when it has ceased to act.

When dogs who have been well house-trained suddenly cease to be so, wanting to draw attention to themselves by voiding urine and/or motions, it is time to give them a dose of *Pulsatilla 200*. This will usually give instant results. If not, a dose of *Platinum 200* is given three days later.

Tiresome battles for supremacy and biting among dogs belonging to one owner can be stopped with *Chamomilla 200*. All the dogs are given a dose at the same time.

Other fears and anxieties may be treated as follows:

Nervousness occurring in the evenings	*Causticum 30*
	Arsenicum album 30,
Fear of being alone	*Phosphorus 30* (barking),
	Pulsatilla 30 (chewing things up)
Fear of men, of trouser legs	*Lycopodium 30*
Fear of anything new	*Argentum nitricum 12x*
Fear during sleep, with barking	*Apis mellifica 3x*, alternating with *Zincum 6x*
Timid, easily frightened	*Kalium phosphoricum 12x*
Consequences of fright	*Opium 30*

Jealousy

A very common failing of man's cherished friend is jealousy. This can certainly cause harm on occasion and should therefore be treated with *Hyoscyamus 200,* once a fortnight. Dogs with a violent temper can also become a danger to those around them, and again it is advisable to give *Hyoscyamus 200* in good time.

Sexual rivalry, common among dogs and also among bitches, will be an indication to an owner who takes his responsibilities seriously that *Platinum 200* is required.

Homesickness

Homesickness causes a dog to lose weight, as he'll be off his food; or to grow hoarse and lose his voice, because he is constantly whining and barking for his 'leader' — his master. Both will make him ill. Everybody knows what a sad sight it is when such an animal returns home from hospital or from a kennel looking desperately thin.

If a dog likely to suffer from homesickness has to be taken to a clinic or to kennels, he should be given two doses of *Ignatia 30* two hours apart just before he is handed over. He will then accept his new surroundings without complaint and will not suffer the pain of separation.

Motion Sickness (Air, Car, Train and Sea Sickness)

It does happen that dogs do not tolerate the forms of transport we use. They may be restless, keep standing all the time and refuse to sit down, yowl and keep rushing from one side of the vehicle to the other. In that case, *Nux vomica 30x* is the remedy.

Otherwise the dog lies down on the floor, salivating or vomiting, and sometimes also voiding involuntarily. *Cocculus 6x* is the remedy for this (in exceptional cases in combination with *Tabacum 6x*).

Both remedies (*Nux* and *Cocculus*) are first given half an hour before the journey starts, and then once an hour. There will be no further need for treatment after a few journeys, as the dog will no longer be prone to the condition.

It is equally effective to give the medication three times daily for ten to fourteen days beforehand.

If it is not travelling as such — travelling at a steady pace on the motorway being well tolerated — but accelerating and braking that causes nausea and vomiting, a single dose of *Strychninum phosphoricum 200* will be highly effective for months, or even for the rest of the dog's life.

Petroleum 200, a single dose once a week, will sometimes also solve the problem, if none of the remedies listed above fit the case.

Epilepsy

The dog suddenly stands stock still, falls to the ground and holds all four limbs out rigidly. After a few seconds convulsions occur, the limbs twitch and move as though the dog were running, the head is twisted round, the eyes are fixed and staring, with the pupils dilated. The animal champs its jaws and there is frothy salivation, stained with blood if he bites his tongue. The bladder is emptied involuntarily.

When the attack is over, the dog walks around in a somewhat dazed state, loss of consciousness having been only temporary. Everything soon returns to normal. The intervals between attacks vary, and it may often be months before this chronic disorder of the brain shows itself again.

During an attack, nothing should be done except to make sure that the dog does not injure himself. Help can be given only during the intervals between attacks, and the following may be considered.

First of all, *Belladonna 6x* should be given every fifteen to thirty minutes soon after the attack, to prevent a repetition. It is repeated attacks at short intervals that make the condition dangerous. They lead to what is known as a status epilepticus, and this can only be stopped by anaesthetizing the dog. Treatment must then be given for some time, four to six months at least.

The dog is given *Cocculus 12x* twice a day, or *Cuprum 30x* and *Oenanthe 30x* once daily in alternation, or *Zincum 6x* alternating with *Apisinum 6x* three times daily; or one can follow the advice of French authors and give the animal *Cuprum 30x* and *Stramonium 30x,* 10 drops of each per day, or *Cuprum 15x* twice daily.

A dose of *Sulphur 200* every two weeks to stimulate reactivity will help recovery. It has to be said, however, that there are congenital and chronic cases where no treatment, homoeopathic or otherwise, will elicit a response.

Seizures or seizure-like states, like attacks of trembling, with foam at the mouth, involuntary voiding of urine, head twisted, lips withdrawn, and the dog falling over, followed by aimless running about, with the dog finally hiding in the dark. If all of this happens within the first seven days after vaccination, *Silicea* will be the remedy. The attacks will then grow less and less marked, like receding waves: *Silicea 12x*, three times daily.

If epileptiform states are triggered by anaesthesia, a dose of *Opium 30* (*x* or *c*) will have a long-term and sometimes even a life-long effect.

Paralysis

Paralysis of the hind quarters may be seen:

> after accidents,
> as a sequel of intervertebral disc disease,
> with distemper when it affects the nervous system, and with osteosis of the spinal meninges in older animals.

Conditions that may mimic paralysis of the hind quarters are severe rheumatic pain in the lumbar region, acute prostatitis, and inflammation of the anal glands.

Any case of paralysis presents its own problems. Mechanical actions such as a blow, a push or an accident may jar the spine, compress it or cause an effusion of blood into it. The paralysis will often only develop hours or even days later.

Arnica 6x can never be given early enough, a dose every one or two hours. If the back is sensitive to being stroked, *Hypericum 3x* should be given in addition.

If the paralysis is due to a prolapsed disc, something seen particularly in Dachshunds who are five to seven years old, *Nux vomica 6x* every two hours throughout the day is the remedy if the paralysis is of the spastic type. This means that the muscles in the hind quarter are tensed and as hard as a board, with pain felt on the least movement. Flaccid paralysis (unless caused by an accident) is treated with *Plumbum metallicum 6x*. This type of paralysis has the characteristic that the muscles begin to atrophy even during the first few days. *Plumbum metallicum* is given every three hours throughout the day, supporting this therapy by producing wheals along the back for two or three days and administration of vitamins E and B12.

Paralysis of the hind quarters may also occur in cases of distemper. The animal is first of all unsteady on its legs, then no longer able to get up from its bed, and finally the paralysis progresses in an anterior direction, sometimes also involving the inspiratory muscles, with, of course, fatal results.

The remedies in these cases are *Conium 6x* and *Cocculus 4x*, both given four times daily.

If the paralysis occurs when complete exhaustion has set in because of the distemper, *Gelsemium 30x*, given twice daily, will be of great value.

Trying to support himself on his front paws, the dog lurches to and fro, finally falling back again. He also finds it difficult to feed, having lost part of his sight through paralysis of the eye muscles, so that his mouth pushes against the side of the bowl. That is *Gelsemium*.

Fortunately, vaccination has made these conditions very uncommon.

Old Alsatians tend to develop paralysis of the hind quarters from one day to the next. This is due to osteosis of the spinal meninges. By giving *Nux vomica 6x* at hourly intervals, it is possible to avoid a paralysis that would otherwise have to end in euthanasia. With *Nux*, the paralysis will pass as quickly as it has appeared. Until the next bout, which may not be until months later, such an old dog will have a good spell free from pain, when he will be able to walk.

Paralysis due to exposure to wet and cold will respond quickly to *Dulcamara 6x*. When muscles become paralysed because of acute rheumatism, which may happen with hunting dogs who have jumped into ice-cold water, *Rhus toxicodendron 6x* (up to *30*) given an alternation with *Bryonia 6x* (up to *30*) will give excellent results, with a dose given every one or two hours, in one of the potencies referred to.

Paralysis, spastic	*Nux vomica 6x*
Paralysis, flaccid	*Plumbum 6x* *Opium 6*
or the following combination: (unless thigh muscles are atrophying)	*Rhus toxicodendron 6x* *Colocynthis 3x* *Gnaphalium 2x $\overline{aa}$* 4-3-2 times daily
Paralysis, sudden, in an old dog	*Nux vomica 6x* hourly
'Paralysis' from cold and damp	*Dulcamara 6x*
'Paralysis' due to rheumatism	*Rhus toxicodendron* or *Bryonia 6x-30*
Paralysis during or after distemper	*Gelsemium 30*

Facial paralysis	*Causticum 6x*
Paralysis following an attack of epilepsy	*Curare 6x-30* *Hypericum* 6th *LM*
Spondylosis, osteochondrosis	*Calcarea fluorica 30x* once a day for two or three weeks

St Vitus' Dance (Chorea), Muscular Twitching, Tic (Myoclonus)

Individual muscle groups twitch involuntarily, and often the whole body shakes. One gets the impression that this is the reaction to a whole series of electrical shocks. The twitching may cease for a time, often during sleep, only to return again in a regular rhythm. This is a long drawn-out illness, very troublesome to the dog and those around him.

Homoeopathy does have a number of remedies to deal with this, and with some patience the dog will soon be able to enjoy life again.

Sedatives clearly have little point in such cases, for the spasms are due to a disorder of the central nervous system, in the brain, usually as a sequel to distemper.

There is however one form of chorea that will quickly respond to treatment. It is the one seen in young dogs who have grown too fast, without the dog necessarily having been subject to distemper. *Phosphorus 30x* is the remedy for this, given once a day until the dog has recovered.

If distemper is the cause, *Agaricus 30x* will give good results in cases where the spasms cease during sleep and are diagonal, i.e. front left and back right, and where one also notices uncoordinated movements when walking, with the hind quarters unusually weak.

Cocculus 6x four times daily is another remedy for this sequel of distemper.

If the spasms do not cease during sleep, *Zincum 6x* will be indicated. *Zincum* has aggravation in the evenings. It is given three times daily.

Leftsided spasms:

    Cuprum, Tarantula

Rightsided spasms:

    Causticum, Arsenicum album

all in the *30x* once a day, or *12x* twice a day.

If none of the above are clearly indicated, the following combination may be used:

> *Calcarea phosphorica 6x*
> *Magnesia phosphorica 6x*
> *Kalium phosphoricum 6x*

three times daily in alternation, continued for some weeks.

Neuralgia

Short-haired breeds are apt to develop neuralgia which usually affects the muscles in the shoulder region. The pain comes on with absolute suddenness and is so tearing that the dog will cry out. The muscles may be swollen, giving the impression that the neck has grown shorter and thicker. The animal moves slowly and stiffly as he walks, and the attacks of pain occur not only when moving but also at rest.

If there is good reason to think that the dog has caught a chill (which need not always be out in the open, but in fact occurs quite frequently through draughts or from lying in front of the door), *Aconitum 6x* will prove miraculously effective. If there is no improvement after a few doses, *Belladonna 6x* will prove the right remedy in most cases. It is given every two hours, until recovery is complete (*Belladonna* is the remedy for local inflammation and spasmodic pain).

A similar condition may be due to a disk lesion in the cervical spine. *Nux vomica 6x* every two hours is the remedy of choice in this case.

If the patient is a bitch of more advanced age, when the ovaries are undergoing involution, *Cimicifuga 4x* or *6x* will prove even more effective.

Roborants, Homoeopathic Tonics

The homoeopathic materia medica includes a number of remedies that do excellent service as tonics and are equal if not superior to the chemical proprietaries used for this purpose. It is important to pay careful attention to the modalities that indicate a particular remedy.

Some examples:

Nux vomica 6x–30x
This is the tonic for people and animals who are irritable and of whom too much has been asked. There is a tendency to constipation and to stomach upsets. *Nux vomica* is an excellent remedy for intoxication (poisoning) and should always be given if this is suspected.

Nux vomica is a very good remedy for treating a dog with a nervous stomach, i.e. a dog who tends to vomit frequently, particularly after a meal, and also eats his vomit immediately afterwards.

In combination with *Carbo vegetabilis* it is very effective in treating all gastrointestinal complaints.

Nux vomica is also the remedy for nervous dogs who for instance get excited when travelling by car, rushing from one side to the other, or keep barking whilst the vehicle is in motion.

Carbo vegetabilis 6x

is outstanding if there is lack or loss of vitality and a marked lack of reactivity.

Zincum 6x

is a roborant particularly for old dogs who are sensitive, losing vitality and getting forgetful. A particular characteristic is marked restlessness and whining.

Kalium phosphoricum 12x

is an excellent remedy for the type of weakness characterized by general irritability and restlessness. Any dog who shows fear will respond to *Kalium phosphoricum 12x* (see under 'Fear and Anxiety', page 111).

Calcarea phosphorica 6x-12x

is the remedy for weakness following acute and chronic illness, and also after nutritional disorders in young dogs. We also always give *Calcarea phosphorica* when dogs are teething (see the relevant chapter) and after bone fractures (see page 79)

If urinalysis shows high phosphate levels, this is always an indication that the organism needs *Calcarea phosphorica 6x* to restore it to normal.

Staphisagria 6x

is a good remedy for nervous animals who get sexually overexcited. It has a calming effect particularly on males if given four or five times daily for some time. *Murex purpurea 6x* will do the same for females.

China 6x

is used to treat weakness after loss of fluids due to diarrhoea, after blood loss, or loss of body fluids due to suppuration and to inflammation of the uterus. These sequelae, when the animal shows weakness and tiredness, are excellent indications for *China*.

There is a special combination that particularly suits older animals who need to be revitalized. To 'rejuvenate' them, we recommend:

Ambra 12x and
Barium carbonicum 12x

once daily for some time, and in addition every four weeks an injection of *Acidum formicicum 30* for slender breeds and types or of *Calcarea carbonica 30* for the opposite type.

In some cases, Nebel's Drainage Remedy[1] may be used as a homoeopathic roborant. This is a combination of several drugs of plant origin in low homoeopathic potency, used to stimulate the excretory organs when prolonged illness has caused the body to be overloaded with toxins. It is often given during convalescence. A similar state also pertains with cancer, and the remedy is then prescribed as an adjuvant before and after surgical removal of the tumour. In cases of inoperable cancer, it is very useful if given in conjunction with *Arsenicum album 6x*. It is also indicated for dogs who will take only meat, so that in the course of some years their one-sided diet has produced a uric acid diathesis. Long-term treatment is advisable, for at least thirty days, giving the remedy between 5 and 7 a.m. and again between 1 and 3 p.m., in accordance with the organic clock of Chinese medicine. The effect will be seen sooner or later, depending on the degree of internal 'pollution'. The treatment may be safely given for longer periods, or repeated after an interval. The composition is *China, Hydrastis canadensis, Solidago virgaurea, Taraxacum, Ceanothus* and *Crataegus 6x* aa.

[1] Obtainable from Jso-Werk, Regensburg, West Germany.

11. Infectious Diseases

Distemper

This is a highly contagious disease affecting young dogs, whatever the breed. The best method of prevention is immunization at ten to twelve weeks. Simultaneous vaccination against up to four diseases is now practised — against distemper, canine virus hepatitis, Stuttgart disease and rabies — and has proved very useful.

Susceptibility to distemper varies. Young dogs are most likely to contract it, but older animals have also been known to get the infection. It is in no way a 'childhood disease'.

The first symptoms are a short-term rise in temperature with tonsillitis, inflammation of the palpebral (eyelid) conjunctiva, and diarrhoea with apathy. They tend to go unnoticed and the disease will already have reached its second stage when after a few days it has advanced so far that it cannot be missed.

Sometimes the only sign that a dog has had distemper during second dentition are the typical 'distemper teeth' (with browny yellow notch-like marks that cannot be removed). The condition may therefore go undetected. There are definitely some hereditary strains with natural immunity where distemper hardly ever develops.

When a young dog has no appetite, is disinclined to move and is apathetic, the temperature should immediately be taken, in the rectum and for two minutes, using an ordinary clinical thermometer with some vaseline applied to the tip. A normal temperature lies between 37.5 and 39°C (99.5 and 102°F); temperatures above 39°C/102°F are febrile.

If there is a temperature, and there are other animals in the house, the dog must be isolated. This may still prevent further infection.

In a case of distemper, other symptoms will soon appear: cough, sneezing, nasal discharge, diarrhoea, conjunctivitis. Occasionally none of these may be seen, and the distemper virus immediately attacks the nervous system, causing encephalitis and convulsions. In these cases there is usually little hope.

There is no specific homoeopathic remedy for distemper. The presenting symptoms must be taken into account, as part of a picture that may change as the disease progresses, requiring further and different remedies.

Treatment must always match the situation.

Diet is of great importance.

Whilst the dog has a temperature, fluids only should be given, choosing those the dog knows already. Boviserin, a bovine blood serum with roborant properties, can also be recommended. It is given by the spoonful, every two or three hours if the dog has no appetite. Egg yolks with glucose and a little red wine, beef broth with egg and lean minced meat, and milk soups are also useful.

Dogs who feed greedily and cannot get enough are usually heading for cerebral congestion (encephalitis). The food needs to be rationed, giving no more than normally, but letting them have plenty to drink. Animals should be taken to their usual places to do their 'business' even when ill, carrying them there if necessary. Short-haired breeds will need a coat or small blanket if it is cold.

Stuttgart Disease

In acute cases this disease is usually fatal. The symptoms are vomiting and diarrhoea, often with blood in both, foetid breath, rapid emaciation, great thirst, severe pain in the lower abdomen, and a high or subnormal temperature.

It is necessary to kill the pathogenic organism quickly, with antibiotics in high doses, despite the fact that *Arsenicum album*, *Mercurius* and *Phosphorus* could easily get it under control. Stuttgart disease is classified as a zoonosis, a disease of animals that may be transmitted to man, presenting problems for the environment, so that antibiotic therapy must be given preference.

The three effective homoeopathic remedies are nevertheless listed below.

Arsenicum album
'Do not consider Arsenic, unless there is restlessness' (Lippe). In the sick dog, this restlessness begins to manifest after midnight when he

will get his owner out of bed because of diarrhoea. Even apart from this he is restless, wandering about all night, or repeatedly changing his resting place. His symptoms meanwhile grow worse. There is a very striking loss of strength in acute illnesses, with rapid exhaustion. The dog looks for warmth, and in acute conditions such as leptospirosis shows marked thirst. He will not drink much at one go, however, but take frequent small drinks instead. The water will often be vomited immediately afterwards. The diarrhoeic stools are black, with a carrion-like offensive smell, and contain blood. With this picture, *Arsenicum album* in any potency will help — *6x, 12x, 30x* or *30*.

Mercurius
Here the tongue is most striking, being thickly coated and furry and showing the imprint of the teeth along its margins (due to swelling of the tongue). The offensive breath, with salivation, redness and sometimes ulceration of the oral mucosa, are further characteristic signs for this remedy. Diarrhoea again is present, being painful, slimy and containing blood, with tenesmus (continual inclination to evacuate the bowels accompanied by painful straining) that persists for a long time and is very troublesome to the dog. The amount of faeces produced is very small.

Phosphorus
Stuttgart disease, with blood in the vomit and bleeding from the intestines, is the domain of *Phosphorus*. A careful observer will note not only trembling weakness, but also numbers of circumscribed areas where the skin is hot, usually between the shoulder blades or along the back. *Phosphorus* also has great thirst. The dog will drink and vomit the water, but only when it has grown warm in the stomach, unlike *Arsenicum album* which has instant vomiting. Other striking symptoms are palpitations and a desire for warmth. As already stated, in acute conditions any potency will help if it is given frequently to begin with (every ten minutes if the dog is haemorrhaging, as this is a dangerous situation), until the condition improves.

These remedies have proved of outstanding value in the treatment of chronic or latent forms of leptospirosis.

Toxoplasmosis

The picture presented by this disease can vary greatly, being sometimes similar to distemper, sometimes like Stuttgart disease, and frequently confused with acute poisoning. In its acute form it may also involve the central nervous system.

The diagnosis is made on the basis of blood tests. However, the Sabin-Feldman dye test will only be positive two or three weeks after infection has occurred. The complement fixation test (CFT) takes even longer to become positive. Acute toxoplasmosis is the diagnosis if both tests are positive.

Apart from frank toxoplasmosis, a condition that is more common than one might think, there are also latent or hidden forms of the disease. These may develop into acute attacks when the organism is subject to stress — due to some other illness, over-exertion or a cold.

Like Stuttgart disease, the condition can also be transmitted to man, by cats and other animals, but never by dogs.

Treatment with the nosode has given good results:

Toxoplasmosis 15x is given once daily, and in addition *Echinacea* mother tincture, 10 drops three times daily, for some weeks.

Epidemic Diarrhoea and Vomiting

Diarrhoea and vomiting call for *Ipecacuanha 6x* every half hour or hour, less frequently as the condition improves. This may be used to treat any kind of diarrhoea and vomiting, including the one due to parvovirus infection (which after all cannot be identified in advance). Parvovirus infection causes sudden onset of violent vomiting, with diarrhoea starting at the same time or just a short time afterwards. The diarrhoea tends to be fast, watery, mixed with blood, and gushing.

As onset and development are very intensive, *Veratrum album 3x* is added to support the circulation, and also *Echinacea 1x*, because there is a rapid drop in white cell count. The combination used to treat rapidly progressing bloody diarrhoea and vomiting thus is:

> *Ipecacuanha 6x*
> *Veratrum album 3x*
> *Echinacea 1x* in equal parts.

10-20 drops are placed directly on the tongue or oral mucosa at fifteen to thirty minute intervals (depending on the situation), increasing the interval between the doses as the condition improves.

This combination should always be at hand, in case of emergency.

Parvovirus infection is dangerous in that dehydration occurs through fluid losses with the diarrhoea and vomiting, and there is also a rapid loss of weight.

When the acute stage is over, *China 6x* is given, a remedy

unsurpassed in restoring strength after fluid loss.

It will obviously also be necessary for the veterinary surgeon to institute further measures once the diagnosis has been established, particularly if the above remedies should not prove effective. There is always the possibility of the condition being due to poisoning, leptospirosis or other causes.

12. Injuries

Treatment of Wounds

Homoeopathic treatment will vary, depending on the nature of the wound.

Contusions with bruising call for *Arnica 4x* and *Hamamelis 3x* in alternation, given at short intervals. *Calendula* ointment is applied externally.

Surgical wounds with poor healing tendencies, abdominal wounds with seroma formation and delayed cicatrization (scar formation) need *Staphisagria 4x*.

Dog bites with tissue loss require *Calendula 2x* internally and, *Calendula* ointment externally.

Suppurating scars or proud flesh are treated with *Staphisagria 4x*. Keloids on the other hand respond well to *Silicea 6x* or *Acidum fluoricum 10x*.

Wounds involving nerve injuries require *Hypericum 3x* internally, once an hour.

Puncture wounds (needles, insect bites) call for *Ledum 4x*.

Torn and wrenched tendons, ligaments and joint injuries require *Ruta 3x* internally and *Calendula* compresses externally.

Cuts will heal better if *Arnica 6x* or *Staphisagria 6x* are given.

Bites and Stings

Puncture wounds are treated with *Ledum 4x* if the degree of pain is much greater than the size of the wound would lead one to expect (otherwise *Arnica* is the remedy), irrespective of whether the puncture was due to a knife, a needle, insect bites, or the stings of wasps and bees.

Externally, *Calendula* ointment is applied, or the wound is bathed with *Calendula* lotion (a teaspoonful of the mother tincture to $\frac{1}{4}$ litre of water).

Dogs running the risk of being stung by bees from a nearby hive every summer should be given a dose of *Apis mellifica 200* at the beginning of the season, to immunize them against bee stings. Such stings will then never be life-threatening, even if a whole swarm of bees were to attack the animal.

Snake bites — in our latitudes specifically from adders — are treated with *Ledum 3x* and *lachesis 8x* in alternation, every fifteen to thirty minutes and less frequently as the condition improves. *Calendula* is also very useful, the tincture in compresses, or the ointment applied to the wound.

Haemorrhages in the eye require *Symphytum 3x;* a 'black eye' — following a blow to the eye — needs *Ledum 4x*, several times a day.

Contusions, e.g. of the paws, need *Hypericum 2x*, an excellent remedy when nerve ends have been injured.

Burns

Echinacea mother tincture, 5–10 drops every hour, is highly effective, rapidly regenerating damaged tissues if the burned skin areas are immediately treated with a compress with well-warmed 70 to 90 per cent alcohol or methylated spirits. For this, some cotton wool soaked in the alcohol or spirits is placed on the wound, covered with a synthetic fabric dressing and a bandage.

If the burns are slight, the compress is left in position for an hour, or if more severe, for up to twelve hours. When the dressing is removed, *Calendula* ointment may be applied if there should be any blisters in evidence. This highly effective treatment for burns may indeed be called homoeopathic, as like is cured with like in this case.

Hypericum oil, Oleum Hyperici, also gives relief of pain and promotes healing with all types of burns. It is very highly regarded because it has great healing powers.

If the dog licks it off, it will not harm the stomach, but will rather act internally as well.

Heat Stroke, Sunstroke

Heat stroke will of course occur only during the hot season, after extreme exertion, and from staying in the heat for too long, e.g. in a parked car. The symptoms will often only show themselves hours later. The animal will then suddenly fall over, lose consciousness, and suffer from difficulties in breathing that are appalling to behold, with a rapid pulse. The tongue and oral mucosa are blue, and there is a high temperature. The eyes stare rigidly, and violent vomiting will often complete the picture, an indication that there is irritation of the brain.

In short, the situation could not be worse. Owners bringing their dog to the surgery usually ask to have him put out of his misery.

The answer is a definite 'No', for we do have a remedy: *Aconitum 6x* (or possibly *Glonoinum 6x*). Given every ten minutes and at longer intervals as improvement sets in, it will soon prove effective. The next day, hardly anyone would think it possible that this happy, healthy creature was the dog who only the day before had been 'stricken' with the heat.

If there are signs of vertigo (dizziness) at a later stage, i.e. the dog lurches and stumbles on getting up, *Gelsemium 6x* will be needed, three times daily for a few days.

Other sequelae are treated with *Natrum carbonicum 15x*, twice daily.

Apis 3x three times daily is indicated with 'cri encephalique', sudden piercing yelps as the blood vessels of the brain are engorged and the meninges become swollen, again in consequence of heat stroke.

Concussion

A fall, a rock fall, or a traffic accident may be responsible for concussion. If this is mild, the dog will stagger or collapse, but soon be on his feet again. In serious cases, he will first vomit and then lose consciousness, with the state of unconsciousness sometimes persisting for quite some time, or even proving fatal. Urine and faeces will be voided involuntarily. The eyeballs may roll, with the pupils greatly dilated. Return to consciousness may be accompanied by convulsions or uncoordinated movements of the limbs, and on occasion the dog may also bite. Absolute quiet and rest are the prime essentials in these cases. The dog is best placed in a darkened room, with cold compresses applied to the head.

Arnica 3x and *Hypericum 6x*, given every fifteen minutes in alternation, have proved very useful in these cases, increasing the intervals between doses as the condition improves. The medication is also given whilst the dog is unconscious, by applying the undiluted drops to the lips or tongue. They will act via the mucous membranes, without having to be swallowed.

If the dog remains unconscious or in a coma for too long, *Opium 6x* is the remedy. We give it once an hour, until the dog wakes up.

Even seemingly very mild forms of concussion — and this includes any accident, even when 'nothing really happened to him' — should be treated with *Arnica 6x* every two hours for some days. This will prevent scar tissue forming in the brain which years later could lead to negative character changes and viciousness.

Late sequelae such as systemic (general) disturbances or convulsions are treated with:

> *Cuprum 15x* in the mornings and
> *Arnica 15x* at night

a single dose, given for some weeks.

Surgical Operations

Arnica is used to prevent excessive blood loss and surgical shock. The *6x* is given several times a day for two days before and after the operation.

If surgical shock develops despite proper care and treatment, and the usual methods will not help, *Phosphorus 30* comes into its own, a few drops or 1 tablet every fifteen minutes until there is improvement.

For post-operative pain, *Hypericum 3x* is given in addition to the *Arnica 3x,* both several times daily.

Severe flatulence (wind) after an operation calls for *Carbo vegetabilis 6x,* several times daily.

Vomiting of food after an operation requires *Ferrum metallicum 30x,* several times daily.

A dynamic ileus and constipation after surgery may be effectively treated with *Staphisagria 6x,* several times daily.

Septic conditions after an operation require *Pyrogenium 15x,* twice daily, or *Pyrogenium 30x,* once daily.

Decubitus (bedsores due to prolonged immobility) are treated with *Silicea 12x* and *Arnica 6x* internally, and *Calendula* ointment applied externally.

Badly healing wounds, suppuration or keloid formation call for *Staphisagria 4x,* several times daily.

13. Poisoning

Boiled or bad meat, fish or sausage

Arsenicum album 6x

Coumarin products, rat poisons that inhibit blood clotting

Lachesis in any potency — *8x, 10x, 30x,* adding vitamin K injections where possible

Toxic symptoms after vaccination, signs of intolerance

Thuja 12x, several times daily

Convulsions after vaccination

Silicea 6th *LM*

A general antidote to all poisons that should be given immediately

Nux vomica 6x

Iron poisoning

Pulsatilla 4x

Lead poisoning

Opium 6x

Poisoning from insecticides, sprays containing DDT, paint and toxic vapours from varnishes or gloss paint, and also as a drainage remedy after severe illnesses

Okoubaka 2x

14. Tumours

Tumours are also on the increase in the animal world. They occur primarily in the mammary lines of bitches, but also in the skin, the mouth, on the thyroid, prostate and testes, around the anus and finally also involving internal organs, in which case they are usually incurable. Even lung cancer is no longer that uncommon nowadays. If surgical removal is undertaken too early, tumour growth tends to be activated. We will therefore usually advise conservative treatment to begin with, using the remedies listed below, and if good fortune is with us, a tumour will often disappear, or at least cease to grow. At this point, surgery may be indicated, with the risk of metastatic spread (from one organ to another) greatly reduced.

Tumours are the outcome of a profound metabolic disorder, and are a secondary symptom of the disease. It is therefore necessary to treat this disorder in the first place, and homoeopaths have some good strings to their bow in this case. Tumour growth is slow and painless as a rule; all one notices is a swelling in the affected site. A tumour is easily distinguished from an abscess, as there is generally no pain and no rise in temperature. Treatment should be initiated as early as possible, for the benefit of the dog as well as those around him. Tumours that are bigger than a chestnut should be surgically removed after prior medical treatment; smaller ones will usually shrink and disappear during treatment.

Tumours of the Breast
These develop after oestrus, and existing tumours tend to increase in size when the bitch has been on heat.
Larger and smaller nodules, as hard as wood, very painful and highly sensitive: *Phytolacca 4x*.

Tumour, stone hard, especially if rightsided, also sequelae of traumas, sensitive and painful: *Conium 10x*.

These are also the principal remedies for fibromas of the breast, which are connective tissue tumours. *Conium 10x* and *Phytolacca 4x-6x*, four times daily in alternation, for several weeks (in the first two weeks, a dose given six times in alternation, later only four times).

Tumours of the jaws, exostoses	*Calcarea fluorica 12x*
	Phosphorus 6x-12x
	Hecla lava 4x-6x
Induration of the prostate (adenoma) depending on the type	*Conium 3x-6x*
	Magnesia carbonica 12x
	Magnesia phosphorica 12x
Induration of the testis (seminoma)	
hard	*Conium 4x*
less hard	*Thuja 6x*
Tumours of the anal sphincter	*Acidum nitricum 6x*
	Thuja 6x
	Arsenicum iodatum 4x
Tumours forming in scars	*Staphisagria 4x*
keloids	*Silicea 6x-12x*
	Acidum formicicum 12x
Basal cell carcinoma of the skin	*Thuja 6x-30x*
Vaginal tumours	*Kreosotum 6x*
Tumours of the breast developing during:	
oestrus	*Phytolacca 4x*
Fibromas	*Calcarea fluorica 12x*
Adenomas	*Conium 6x* with
	Phytolacca 4x
Hard tumours of the thyroid	*Conium* in *LM* potencies

Thyroid tumours that are not hard   *Thuja* in *LM* potencies
(not to be confused with goitre, which requires *Calcarea iodata 4x*)

Inoperable tumours are treated with the constitutional remedy (see Chapter 17). If this cannot be determined, *Arsenicum album 6x* three times daily will help, relieving the pain and improving the general condition, though it will not effect a cure.

15. Causative Factors

Fright or shock — *Opium 30* (single dose)

Awkward movement, especially Dachshunds, also if followed by paralysis — *Rhus toxicodendron 12x* / *Nux vomica 6x* / *Arnica 6x*

New home, homesickness, mourning a lost master — *Ignatia 30* (three doses in one day)

Vaccination (local) — *Thuja 12x*

Mental sequelae; convulsions — *Silicea 12x*

Loss of much blood or other body fluids — *China 6x*

Suppressed skin eruptions — *Sulphur 12x-30x*

Getting wet through — *Rhus toxicodendron 12x*, *Dulcamara 4x-6x*

Too much convenience food (dry or tinned) — *Natrum muriaticum 12x*

Oestrus (tumour growth) — *Phytolacca 4x*

Excitement (diarrhoea) — *Argentum nitricum 12x*

These remedies are given three times daily, in the potencies stated, until the condition improves.

16. Eugenic Treatment

This is given mainly prior to birth, to improve the hereditary characteristics and the health of the as yet unborn.

During pregnancy, the bitch is given high potencies of individually selected remedies, at specific intervals. These will improve the hereditary characteristics in so far as morbid dispositions that caused disease in the parents and grandparents will not be passed on. It is possible to achieve effective prevention of some of the diseases to which certain strains tend to be subject:

Skeletal deformation, connective tissue weakness, mental disorders, disorders affecting the coat etc. — it is a wide field.

It is necessary to review the diseases to which earlier generations, or at least both parents, have been subject, classify them, and design a course of treatment with profoundly acting antipsoric remedies that will then result in the new generation being born with no or only minimal predisposition to these diseases. It is a very worthwhile method, especially for breeders wishing to improve a breed, though it will not always take full effect with the first litter. One has to think in terms of generations, albeit the rather short-lived generations of dogs.

The opportunities offered by eugenics are truly great. Treasures await those who are prepared to go for them.

It must again be stressed that eugenic therapy is highly individual, and it requires an expert to create the right composition of high potencies, based on the predispositions and diseases of previous generations. It may also be mentioned that selected high potencies can be used to achieve 'homoeopathic immunization' against infectious diseases.

This is an extremely complex and multi-layered field, where considerable research still has to be done.

It is however already possible to state the following:

A single dose each of:

Sulphur 200
Calcarea carbonica 200
Tuberculinum 200
Distemperinum 200

one after the other at three-day intervals at the beginning of pregnancy, will produce a litter that is in far better condition than any preceding one.

This treatment is given to a bitch only once in her life, irrespective of how many times she is mated and gives birth.

It is of course possible to vary and individualize this treatment, but that would require extensive study and preparation, taking into account the diseases of previous generations, and cannot be discussed here in more detail. It is a specialist field for veterinary surgeons who are homoeopaths, requiring a great deal of experience.

17. Some Constitutional Types

Acidum formicicum (formic acid)
The drug picture of *Acidum formicicum* demonstrates how closely the provings (symptoms produced by healthy subjects given the substance in homoeopathic potencies) on humans and animals resemble each other, so that human drug pictures can indeed be used in veterinary medicine.

Dog	Man
Striking apathy and tiredness.	General weakness and inability to perform (work). Rheumatic pain in limbs, starting on right and progressing to left, then moving back again.
Sudden onset of rheumatic complaints.	Highly sensitive to wet and cold, cold baths, which aggravate. Sudden onset of rheumatic complaints.
Aggravation from movement, yet desire to move.	Aggravation from movement, yet desire to move, better from pressure.
Very lively, wanting to play, once symptoms have gone.	Inclined to catch colds, enhanced faculty for work, very lively, enjoys work - great sensation of weakness.
Not interested in surroundings, lies down	Mood variable and irritable, cheerful — depressed and grouchy, dwells on

in a dark place, does not respond when called — very attached and needing to be loved.

old hurts, long since done with, and old injuries and affairs long since past.
Feeling of anxiety, as if some disaster were about to happen.

Feeble, apathetic, frequent yawns and stretching of limbs.

Rush of blood to the head, persistent pressing pain in the head, stabbing pain in the forehead, with dizziness and nausea, tired brain, poor memory, sleepy, frequent yawning and stretching of limbs.

No appetite or thirst.

Catarrh with coryza, hoarseness and cough. Violent bouts of coughing with vomiting, dyspnoea with desire for fresh air.
Inflamed gums, throat and palate very much reddened, pain in palatal arch, when swallowing.

Diarrhoea in small quantities, black, frequently with tenesmus

Catarrhal gastritis and enteritis, with the usual symptoms and much flatulence.

Blood in the urine, groans when passing water.

Haematuria with pressive pains in the urethra and in the gut. Urine contains blood and protein, stinking, concentrated urine, marked urgency.
Pollution and voluptuous dreams. Menses start eight days early, sparse and pale, with sensation of uterus pressing down.

Striking muscular weakness, when picked up, whole body hangs down limply.
Spasmodic twitching and contraction of individual muscle groups when back

Striking muscular weakness.
Rheumatoid pains in all extremities: stiffness, lightning pains, hands humming, spasmodic twitching and contraction of individual muscle groups. Lumbago-type pain, with aggravation from cold and wet.

is stroked. Lumbago-type pain. Stiffness, with sudden yelps. Desire for movement although obviously in pain, particularly at night (duration of up to eight days).

Desire for movement although this aggravates pain, better from pressure. Itching of scalp, skin on trunk and extremities. (Duration of fourteen to twenty-one days.)

Arnica

How does *Arnica* act? What kind of drug picture, or combination of symptoms, does it produce if given to healthy humans or animals?

Dog

Man

Won't let himself be touched without making defensive movement. Location of pain not clearly defined.

Hypersensitivity of whole body. Afraid of being touched even as one approaches. Pain on any movement or when touched.

Exhausted, as though after a thorough beating (*rouer de coups*)

Sore feeling all over, as if beaten. Great weakness and exhaustion. Weariness. Worse from touch and movement. Better lying down and at rest.
Painful sensitivity of all joints on least movement. Muscles and joints are sore as if bruised.

Skin and mucosa more or less inflamed, generally no actual wounds.

Rush of blood to the head, with limbs cold, due to venous congestion. Frequent nosebleeds, head colds. Cough, with sensation as if ribs were broken. Cough with irritation deep down in the trachea.

Nausea
Salivation
Vomiting
'All the symptoms of gastroenteritis with diarrhoea'.

Head feels dazed, with dizziness when head is moved. Headache worse from cough and bending down. Internal and external heat of head and face. Pressive headache when walking, climbing stairs,

thinking, reading. Pulse accelerated, palpitations, stabbing and pressive pains in the heart. Unbearable precordial angor, sensation as if heart would cease to beat. Cardiac oppressions.
Halitosis. Bitter eructations. Griping stomach pains. Bloated abdomen. Offensive flatus. Colicky pain in abdomen. Involuntary stools at night during sleep. Diarrhoea with slimy, purulent, bloody stools. Stools consisting of mucus only.

Nervous excitation particularly of the spinal marrow, shows trembling and 'convulsions', soon followed by weariness, and loss of muscle power with general loss of sensation.

Highly excitable mentally in an acceptable as well as an unacceptable way. Indifferent to everything, depressed, hopeless, nervous, easily frightened.
Fear of both present and future. Does not say a word. Obstinate and contentious, whatever you do is wrong. Absent and dazed. Incapable of mental effort. Loss of memory. Drowsiness.

In cases of traumatic injury or accident we give intensive *Arnica* therapy, using the *3x*, with 5 drops placed on the tongue every five or ten minutes, increasing the interval to one, two and three hours as the condition improves. This achieves not only early relief of pain, but also rapid recovery, avoiding complications.

Dog bites are treated surgically where necessary, and at the same time a *Calendula* compress (20 drops of the tincture to a glass of boiled water) or *Calendula* ointment is applied — its virtues are beyond praise — and covered with a dressing.

This treatment will make antibiotics and sulphonamides unnecessary.

Professional breeders or dealers may not always have the time to give frequent doses of the low potency and will find it easier to place 5 granules of *Arnica 30* on the tongue two or three times daily.

Arsenicum album
Emaciation and weakness, yet also fear and restlessness in some form.

Aggravation after midnight, between 1 and 3 a.m., either itching and scratching, or restlessly running to and fro in the house, needing to go out if there is diarrhoea.

Frequent but small drinks, often vomiting the water again immediately afterwards.

Black diarrhoea, smells offensive, often also containing blood. Sensitive anus.

Extremities cold, skin dry, flaking, with itching eczema all over the body.

Ignatia

Ignatia is the female counterpart to the *Nux vomica* type which generally is more suited to males.

The *Ignatia* type is nervous, irritable, hysterically anxious, easily frightened, inclined to cramps and spasms. Typical female habit, may also be found in male animals who impress one as being feminine. Remarkable variability of mood, swinging from one extreme to the other. As a result these animals are unpredictable. They yowl and moan, and are beside themselves even over little things, upset and ill-tempered. At the same time they are extremely easily frightened.

Cannot bear noise, and will, if possible, withdraw to a quiet place.

Being sensitive to cold, they will look for warm spots in the home; they like going under the bed covers, or being covered up in their baskets. Aggravation of all symptoms from physical exertion, from excitement, fright and fear, and from touch, cold, tobacco smoke and sweet things.

All symptoms particularly marked in the mornings, gradually improving as the day goes on.

Gentle movement, external warmth and gentle pressure, on the other hand, are welcomed by these animals.

Lycopodium

Among dogs, as among humans, there are also fat, indolent types with hepatic insufficiency.

Ravenously hungry, but cannot make a good meal, for he feels 'full' after just a few mouthfuls and turns away. It will be evening before he'll take a little food — if any — so that he'll lose weight in the long run.

Extremely irritable and hot-tempered, scarcely able to bear being trained. When his master tries to tell him off or even punish him, the dog will turn on him and attempt to bite.

Black marks develop in abdominal skin with old age (*Sepia* has brown marks). Type of uric acid diathesis. Organism overloaded with uric acid which becomes deposited in the long muscles of the back, particularly in the sacral region.

Natrum muriaticum

Your *Natrum muriaticum* dog will never come leaping up to you, the way the playful *Phosphorus* type does. And it *will* be never — for *Natrum muriaticum* tends to be shy, withdrawn, reserved, not very sociable, and certainly does not like strangers. If after much coaxing one finally wants to pet him, he will not refuse immediately, and will let himself be patted once or twice, but then he will bite, suddenly getting annoyed. He will only give a nip usually, but it is enough to give him a reputation of being tricky.

He also likes to attack other dogs, but if he realizes that this will not achieve anything he will make a conciliatory move and return to his master. One may call this cautious, or cowardly.

In veterinary practice, the *Natrum muriaticum* picture will be seen in animals who have been given the wrong diet, being in part due to that diet. The type is frequently seen in pubs and restaurants where the animals are fed on leftovers, and also when owners feed them entirely on tinned dog foods, giving preference to one particular brand. If you have a *Natrum muriaticum* type on the table in your surgery, the first thing you notice is the lack-lustre, dull, sometimes rough coat. If you run your hand over it, you will end up with a fistful of hair. Pruritus and eczema in the axillae and joint flexures are not uncommon, these being the preferred sites for skin conditions with the type. It is also obvious that the dog likes having his back firmly massaged. Firm pressure clearly does him good, and he will be wagging his tail. The next thing one notes are the cold ears, cold extremities, and altogether a lack of vital warmth. These dogs rarely have a high temperature. On the other hand they frequently show great thirst, and a desire for highly seasoned foods and for salt. Their craving will be such that they will lick the sweaty hands of those around them, and particularly also their feet if going barefoot.

When the *Natrum muriaticum* dog comes home from a walk he will first of all rush to his water bowl. The type is not always lean and slender; some are indeed fat and bloated and, as already mentioned, highly irritable. These dogs will bark at any sound, and make no clear distinction between friend and foe, which limits their usefulness as watchdogs.

A very striking feature is that they very rapidly get tired. Compared to *Phosphorus* who is sparkling with life, getting exhausted in the exhilaration of movement or of play, the *Natrum muriaticum* dog will be gasping for breath, his heart rate increased, after every minor effort. His battery is never more than half charged. He will sleep whenever possible. The chilliness of *Natrum muriaticum* animals is in a class of its own. It is amazing to hear how close to the radiator or heater they will lie — one would think they must be getting burned. And what a job it is to get them to go out in the street when it is cold and raining.

Natrum muriaticum can be spotted from the fact that he will avoid the sun. These animals immediately pull whoever is walking them into the shade. Dogs who like to laze about in the sun, visibly enjoying it and possibly even going to sleep, can never be classified as *Natrum muriaticum*. They are also very much inclined to harbour resentment, remembering any wicked deed done to them for a long time afterwards.

Lacrimation is almost always present. The discharge will only for a time respond to eye-drops. The continuous chronic discharge will cause a channel to form. Discharges, when they occur, have the appearance of white of egg, an indication for *Natrum muriaticum* in many cases of metritis (inflammation of the uterus).

Phosphorus

The most obvious sign: cannot bear to be alone. Left on his own he will howl, whine and bark. He wants company, wants variety, wants to be talked to, and to play with children.

The next striking sign: if a thunderstorm is approaching, he will have come to hide somewhere near a person in his fear.

He totally dislikes the changes in atmospheric electricity, particularly during the preceding hours, and also all loud noises. Some *Phosphorus* dogs will in fact overcompensate for their sensitivity to loud noises, by running towards a clap of thunder. Another way in which they often overcompensate for their fear is by biting.

As for training, this becomes an endless trial of patience with this type. These dogs are too playful and cannot concentrate. It is really difficult to teach them anything. Nor is it exactly easy to get them house-trained. Sometimes they seem extremely tense, as though wound up. They may jump up against a door handle twenty or thirty times, to open it. They are also very curious and fidgety.

Walking on a lead, such a dog will almost burst with curiosity and nervousness, always pulling strongly on the lead, even when wearing a training collar. He would rather throttle himself than stop pulling, dragging his owner, who after all does not want to let him get throttled, all the way after him.

Bursting with temperament, the *Phosphorus* dog nevertheless likes to take a break now and then after exertion; he is easily exhausted, but soon bounces back again after a short rest.

The frame is slender and delicately boned (in humans, this would be the leptosome type). The coat is fine and silky, with little pigmentation, thin-skinned, normally with a light-coloured coat.

The veins stand out strongly on the extremities, particularly the hind legs.

The head is long, examples being that of a Setter, or of Lassie, the Border Collie who achieved fame on television. Analogous to this, *Phosphorus* types will of course be found in any breed, even among Bull Terriers and the normally very short-nosed Pekinese.

The dog will have an appetite at any time. Food is burned up quickly, and he will be able to take more food even after a good meal. No one knows where he puts it. Stools more than the food he has eaten.

It may also be the case, every homoeopathic remedy being biphasic, that the *Phosphorus* dog takes no food whatsoever during the day, but then makes up for this at night. However, not every dog who feeds at night is also a *Phosphorus* type. *China, Lycopodium* and *Psorinum* also have marked hunger at night.

There is another important combination of symptoms often seen in *Phosphorus* dogs: they sometimes appear to have a stabbing sensation in the anus, itching, formication, and perhaps also burning in the anus, analogous to the symptoms noted in man. In a dog it takes the form that the animal is chasing its own tail, seemingly in play, running around in circles, and biting into the root of the tail if this can be reached. When marked, this is a one hundred per cent reliable indication for *Phosphorus,* even if it happened only in the past, when the dog was young.

Sexual drive is considerably above average, and may at times be abnormally so. Yet although the fire burns so brightly, it usually proves a mere flash in the pan — the dog is impotent, particularly as he is also prone to masturbate. Oestrus is greatly extended in bitches, who will sometimes bleed for three or four weeks instead of the normal ten or twelve days.

You could identify a *Phosphorus* dog on the table even with eyes blind-folded, just by touch. His heart will always be going extremely rapidly as he is picked up and placed on the table, and he generally tends to have violent palpitations on these and similar occasions. Indeed, one can hear his heart beating from a distance. Moving one's hands over his coat one can clearly identify skin areas that are much warmer, usually between the shoulder blades, but also in other places — areas the size of the palm of one's hand that are warmer than the surrounding areas. The dog will also be extremely ticklish and therefore restless and extremely nervous during the examination.

Phosphorus 200 has been recommended for nervous people prior to a medical examination, and we also like to use this remedy when dealing with nervous animals.

Emphasis must be given to the inclination to haemorrhage with a *Phosphorus* patient. All the mucous membranes will bleed easily: kidneys, bladder, stomach, intestines, — vomit and also stools will very easily contain blood. When cystitis does not respond easily to *Belladonna* or *Cantharis, Phosphorus* will be indicated, and also when there is haemorrhage with inflammation, in gastritis and gastroenteritis.

A *Phosphorus* dog will frequently cough for no apparent reason when there is a change from warm to cold, or from cold to warm, also for nervous reasons, joy and excitement, though no diagnosis can be made.

These dogs also have a musical peculiarity that will be found with no other remedy: they will howl when hearing sounds of a certain pitch, e.g. the whistle of a kettle or the ringing of bells.

Phosphorus has a most peculiar sensitivity to its own offensive smells. Dogs will usually take a very interested sniff at the secretion from their own anal glands when this has been expressed, as happens occasionally. A *Phosphorus* dog will turn away with an expression of disgust, and would really like to run away.

When one has a *Phosphorus* type, but this must always be very clearly marked, *Phosphorus* should in case of illness always be given in high potency first, using other indicated remedies in low potency to deal with local symptoms. But usually, unless there has been an accident or an epidemic disease, i.e. a disease due to external causes, one will find all his symptoms in the drug picture, and he will almost always present with a *Phosphorus* disease.

Sepia

The female *Sepia* type will consistently bite and drive away any male during the fertile period, when the bleeding of oestrus has stopped. Mating will be possible only by using force, holding the bitch, and this in turn tends to lead to birth complications.

In these cases, *Sepia 6x* needs to be given for about three weeks before they are due to come on heat, preferably three times daily.

The type is dark-haired, and like *Lycopodium* develops patches of dark discoloration in the skin of the abdomen when older.

Sepia, too, is not exactly pleasant company, but not nearly as unfriendly as *Natrum muriaticum.*

The type does not like small children or young dogs.

Sulphur
Sulphur produces diseases that are interrelated with skin eruptions. It is the remedy of choice for conditions (of any kind) where new skin eruptions will come up as the condition improves.

The type smells of sulphur. There is redness of orifices – eyes, mouth, tongue, vagina, anus, all show increased redness. The dog is not fat, nor is he lean, the hair is dry, rough, without lustre. Eczemata tend to be dry, itching particularly at night, and are only rarely of the moist type.

He has an aversion to having a bath and will steer well clear of water. Tends to be constipated, but frequently also has diarrhoea. Constipation and diarrhoea in one and the same motion are a very clear indication for *Sulphur*. Morning diarrhoea, driving him and his owner out into the street, and then no further stools at all for the rest of the day.

Graphites
Graphites is overweight, fat, chilly, constipated with a tendency to dry, fissured or weeping skin eruptions, particularly in skin folds, with honey-like, sticky secretions.

This fat, anxious and phlegmatic type has a striking sensitivity to cold. Feels very much better when covered with a blanket.

Also cracked claws, sometimes overlarge and malformed. Rhagades at the corner of the mouth and in the anus. Discharge from ear smelling of herring brine.

Itching around the anus, the dog will slide, 'go tobogganing', although he does not have worms or an inflammation of the anal glands.

Sensitive areas are those of transition from skin to mucosa. Dry or moist eczema in the joint flexures, loss of hair behind the ears. Fungus infections, particularly in the claw bed and between the toes. Small, often very painful fissures at the nostrils.

The appetite is always good, and he will even eat in advance, to have something in store. Meat is not a priority with him. Much flatulence with offensive flatus. Stools often covered in white mucus.

Pulsatilla
The *Pulsatilla* type is capricious, mild, gentle, yielding, obedient, affectionate, and sad and depressed on the days preceding oestrus. (The majority of *Pulsatilla* types are female.)

Being on his own is not one of his strong points; he does not actually bark (as *Phosphorus* does), but will chew up everything in sight. Each time his master returns he is greeted with much enthusiasm as though he had been away for weeks, yet it may only have been minutes.

Does not tolerate fats and sweets, nor anything really cold, which will cause immediate diarrhoea, mixed with mucus and constantly changing in both colour and consistency. No one stool is like another.

All secretions are thick and yellow, and also somewhat slimy, irrespective of whether the discharge is from the eye or the uterus.

Muscular and joint pains are better from movement and in the open air, whilst rest and warmth aggravate.

Skin problems and pruritus are of hormonal origin and usually develop at night, with small red pustules and vesicles.

It is worth noting that these dogs often feel cold and have cold paws, which can easily lead to colds if they get wet through.

A lovable creature, not exactly brave; phlegmatic and inclined to whimper, with depressive phases due to hormonal causes — that, on the whole, is *Pulsatilla.*

18. Alphabetical Index of Remedies

Abrotanum
(southernwood)

Lack of appetite, or ravenous and losing weight, diarrhoea alternating with constipation, whelps with worms.

Acidum formicicum
(formic acid)

Predisposition to rheumatic and allergic conditions, uric acid diathesis, alterative and regenerative actions.

Acidum nitricum
(nitric acid)

Affinity to mucous membranes at transition from skin to mucosa, around the mouth, nose, urethra and anus. Ulcers, fissures, 'pongy dog' remedy.

Acidum sulphuricum
(sulphuric acid)

Remedy for nervous system, blood and mucous membranes, heartburn.

Aconitum napellus
(aconite, monkshood)

All inflammatory states of sudden onset, starting with a temperature and vascular embarrassment, caused by exposure to cold, particularly a north wind. Anxiety, restlessness, panting. Initial stages of febrile conditions and inflammatory states.

Aesculus hippocastanum
(horse chestnut)

Inflammation of anal gland, phlebitis.

Aethiops antimonialis
(mercury and antimony
sulphides)

Colitis.

Agaricus muscarius
(fly agaric)

St Vitus' dance.

Agnus castus
(chaste tree)

Increased libido.

Alumina
(pure clay)

Constitutional inferiority of mucous
membranes, constipation. Paralysis of
bladder and rectum.

Ambra grisea
(ambergris)

Nerve tonic, remedy for problems of
ageing.

Antimonium arsenicosum

Bronchitis, persistent cough,
congestion in pulmonary circulation.

Antimonium crudum
(sulphide of antimony)

Gastric complaints following
unsuitable foods, lack of appetite,
tongue coated, nails do not grow
properly, corns and calluses, skin
cracks, hyperkeratoses, warts.

Antimonium tartaricum
(tartar emetic)

Cough producing mucus, febrile
bronchitis, bronchopneumonia,
pneumonia.

Apis mellifica
(honey bee)

Inflammation and swelling of skin
and mucous membranes, urticaria,
inflammation of the bladder and
kidney, rheumatism, sore throat.

Argentum nitricum
(silver nitrate)

Conditions affecting the mucous
membranes, nervous diseases, greedy
for sugar and sweets, which are not
tolerated.

Aristolochia clematitis
(birthwort)

Correction of hormonal imbalance,
treatment of wounds.

Arnica montana
(arnica)

Consequences of mechanical injuries,
contusions, sprains, bruises, muscular
pain after major exertions,
overstrained heart, myocardial
weakness, and alternating with

Belladonna as first aid treatment following a stroke.

Arsenicum album
(white oxide of arsenic)

Asthma, chilliness, ascites, diarrhoea, eczema, gastroenteritis, pneumonia, cancer, emaciation and exhaustion, restlessness and fear.

Burning pain in dry skin. Great thirst, but only takes small quantities. Dry eczema, nephritis, often with diarrhoea and vomiting. Remedy for terminal stage of cancer, aggravation after midnight, better from warmth.

Aurum metallicum
(gold)

Keratitis with reticulum of veins on the cornea. Constitutional remedy for full-blooded breeds such as Boxers, Pugs and dogs of similar habit.

Baryta carbonica
(barium carbonate)

Sebaceous cysts, chronic tonsillitis in young dogs, remedy for ageing dogs suffering from vertigo, an ageing heart and arteriosclerosis.

Belladonna
(deadly nightshade)

Febrile conditions with mastitis and orchitis.

Pulmonary congestion, cerebral congestion, stroke, aggressiveness.

Remedy for acute local inflammation, follows the *Aconitum* stage.

Bellis perennis
(daisy)

Consequences of injuries and over-exertion. Feeling of exhaustion and soreness all over, also in the uterus.

Berberis
(barberry)

Remedy for liver, gall bladder and kidney conditions, uric acid diathesis, urinary gravel and calculi, renal colics, follow-up treatment with Stuttgart disease, hepatorenal syndrome.

Borax	Hypersensitivity to sounds and great noise.
Bryonia alba (white bryony, wild hops)	Bronchitis with dry cough, pneumonia, pleuritis, vomiting of bile, jaundice, mastitis, acute rheumatism.
Cactus grandiflorus (night-blooming cereus)	Cardiac weakness, ageing heart.
Calcarea carbonica Hahnemannii (middle of oyster shell)	Constitutional remedy for heavy-headed types, perverse appetites, rickets, epilepsy, goitre, lipoma, warts.
Calcarea fluorica (calcium fluoride)	Cataract, rickets, dental problems, connective tissue weakness, periostitis, bone diseases.
Calcarea phosphorica	Demineralization, eclampsia, epilepsy, rickets, growth disorders in slender types.
Calculi biliarii (gall stones)	Gall stones, splenic calculi.
Calendula (marigold)	Disinfection of wounds, bruises, suppurating lesions, insect bites. External use as an ointment or a mixture of 1–2 teaspoons of the tincture to $\frac{1}{4}$ litre of water, also undiluted for inflammation of the auditory canal and eczema of the lips.
Cantharis (Spanish fly)	Irritated state of bladder and urethra, cystitis, nephritis, burns, dermatitis with vesiculation.
Carbo vegetabilis (charcoal)	Perverse appetite, flatus, halitosis.
Carduus marianus (Marian thistle)	Hepatitis and cirrhosis of the liver.
Causticum Hahnemannii (caustic)	Nervous bladder, remedy for warts, weakness of hind quarter(s) and

gradually developing lameness.

Ceanothus
(red root)

Diseases of the spleen.

Cephaelis ipecacuanha
(Ipecacuanha)

Bronchitis, gastritis with vomiting, enteritis with bloody diarrhoea.

Chamomilla
(chamomile)

Diarrhoea when teething, gripes, convulsions, toothache.

Chelidonium majus
(greater celandine)

Hepatic failure, jaundice; relieves spasm in gastro-intestinal complaints.

China
(Peruvian bark)

States of exhaustion following loss of blood or other fluids through diarrhoea, vomiting etc. anaemia.

Chininum arsenicosum
(quinine arsenite)

As for *China* and *Arsenicum album*.

Cimicifuga
(black cohosh)

Rheumatism in the muscles of the neck, hormonal imbalance in older bitches (climacteric).

Cinnabaris
(mercuric sulphide)

Mycosis, chronic sinus disease.

Clematis

Prostatitis, orchitis.

Cocculus
(Levant nut)

Travel sickness.

Colocynthis
(bitter cucumber)

Sudden colics, meteorism (distention of intestines by gas), flatulence.

Conium maculatum
(hemlock)

Testicular eczema, vertigo in old age, glandular indurations, tumours.

Crataegus
(hawthorn)

Senile heart with palpitations, cardiovascular stimulant.

Cuprum metallicum
(copper)

Convulsions, twitching of extremities, paroxysmal cough, suffocating cough.
  Cuprum oxydatum nigrum 4x is a remedy for worms, similar to *Abrotanum*.

Cyclamen europaeum
(wild cyclamen)

Pseudopregnancy.

Damiana (Turnera aphr.)	Impotence.
Digitalis purpurea (foxglove)	Oedema of prostate, heart conditions.
Dulcamara (Solanum dulc., bittersweet)	Rheumatism after getting wet through, cystitis. Nervous bladder.
Echinacea angustifolia (cone flower, Rudbeckia)	Infections, wounds, septicaemia, tonsillitis. To enhance the defensive powers. Externally in the form of ointment or a solution of 1 or 2 teaspoons of the tincture in $\frac{1}{4}$ litre of water.
Euphrasia officinolis (eyebright)	Blepharitis, inflammation of cornea and lacrimal duct.
Ferrum metallicum (iron)	Loss of appetite alternating with normal feeding. Anaemia.
Ferrum phosphoricum (phosphate of iron)	Fever, onset of congestive illnesses.
Flor de Piedra (stone flower)	Liver conditions.
Gelsemium sempervirens (yellow jasmine)	Meningeal irritation, heat stroke, paralysis of hind quarters as a sequel to distemper with cerebral congestion.
Graphites (black lead)	Moist eczema, fissures and cracks in the skin, inflammation of auditory canal with catarrh, secretions 'like honey', remedy for scars (like *Sepia*).
Hamamelis (witch hazel)	Seeping haemorrhages, haemorrhages from bladder.
Hecla lava (lava from Mount Hecla in Iceland)	Tumours in the region of the jaw. Periostitis.
Helonias dioica (false unicorn root)	Uterine tonic.

Hepar sulphuris
(sulphur)

Low potencies promote pus, high potencies will inhibit it, abscesses, boils, suppurating glands, patient hypersensitive to touch, pain and cold. Anything involving suppuration.

Hydrastis canadensis
(golden seal)

Remedy for mucous membranes, particularly of the uterus.

Hyoscyamus
(henbane)

Aggressiveness, hysterical excitement, jealousy, paralysis, dry spasmodic cough, nervous bladder.

Hypericum
(St John's wort)

Nerve injuries, paralysis. Oil of Hypericum is an excellent vulnerary (wound remedy), also for burns and abrasions.

Ignatia
(St Ignatius' bean)

Homesickness remedy.

Iodum
(iodine)

Goitre, emaciation though appetite still normal.

Kalium phosphoricum
(potassium phosphate)

Nervousness, anxiety, states of exhaustion.

Kreosotum
(creosote)

Conditions affecting skin and mucosa, with offensive smell.

Lachesis
(surukuku snake poison)

Gangrenous tonsillitis, jealousy, septicaemia, metritis. Infectious diseases with blood poisoning, phlegm.

Ledum palustre
(Labrador tea)

Insect bites, rheumatism of muscles and joints, gout.

Lithium carbonicum
(lithium carbonate)

Stones in the bladder.

Lycopodium
(club moss)

Chronic hepatic insufficiency, loss of appetite, pneumonia.

Magnesia carbonica
(carbonate of magnesia)

Symptoms due to renal calculi, gout, rheumatic diathesis, spasms, enlarged prostate.

Magnesia phosphorica
(phosphate of magnesia)

Spasms and colics, constipation with stools dry, like sheep dung.

Mercurius solubilis
(mercury)

Inflammation of the mucosa of the mouth and gastrointestinal tract, sore throat, gingivitis, colitis, diseases of salivary gland, jaundice, inflammation of auditory canal, peritonitis, nephritis.

Millefolium
(yarrow)

Tendency to haemorrhage.

Murex purpurea
(glandular secretion from a mollusc)

Sexual excitement in female animals, jealousy.

Myristica sebifera
(nutmeg species)

The 'homoeopathic scalpel', promotes liquefaction of purulent processes such as abscesses.

Natrum muriaticum
(common salt)

Emaciation, loss of hair, chronic blepharitis, cataract.

Natrum sulphuricum
(sodium sulphate)

Jaundice.

Nux vomica
(poison nut)

Loss of appetite, nervous stomach disorders, excess gastric acid, constipation, colic.

Okoubaka
(African bark)

Alimentary poisoning.

Opium
(poppy)

Coma, constipation, consequences of shock or fright.

Petroleum
(coal or rock oil)

Eczema, rhagades, fissures.

Petroselinum
(parsley)

Nervous bladder.

Phosphorus
(yellow phosphorus)

Nervous exhaustion, diarrhoea, internal bleeding, jaundice, Stuttgart disease, pneumonia, inflammation and infection of bones.

Phytolacca decandra
(poke root)

Mastitis, tumours of the breast.

Platinum	Jealousy. Excessive libido.
Plumbum metallicum (lead)	Constipation, flaccid paralysis, muscular atrophy.
Podophyllum (American mandrake)	Gushing stools (hydrant).
Psorinum (nosode)	Inflammation of auditory canal, eczema in winter, chronic mycosis (fungus infection).
Pulsatilla (pasque flower)	Purulent catarrh with secretions bland, not excoriating, gastritis, pseudopregnancy, orchitis, inflammation of auditory canal, blepharitis.
Pyrogenium (putrid matter — beef)	Severe, febrile infections, septicaemia.
Rhus toxicodendron (poison ivy)	Cystitis, eczema, paralysis, rheumatism.
Ruta graveolens (rue)	Contusions, over-exertion, sprains, periosteum, strained tendons.
Sabal serrulata (saw palmetto)	Prostatitis and enlarged prostate.
Secale cornutum (ergot)	Uterine inertia, lack of muscle tone in uterus.
Sepia (cuttlefish)	Metritis, hormonal imbalance in older bitches.
Serum anguillae (eel serum)	Chronic nephritis with massive albuminuria.
Silicea (pure silica)	Cold abscesses, cataract, epilepsy, fistules, chronic suppuration.
Solidago virgaurea (golden rod)	Kidney and bladder remedy.
Spongia tosta (roasted sponge)	Asthma, induration of testes, goitre, nervous cough.
Stannum (tin)	Chronic bronchitis.

Staphisagria (stavesacre)	Sexual overexcitement, suppuration from scars, keloids.
Sticta pulmonaria (lungwort)	Nervous cough, bronchitis.
Sulphur (brimstone, flowers of sulphur)	Skin eruptions, dandruff, constipation, morning diarrhoea, eczema, chronic diseases, aids regeneration after illness.
Sulphur iodatum (sulphur iodide)	Inflammation of lymph glands, enlarged tonsils.
Tabacum (tobacco)	Travel sickness.
Tartarus emeticus	see *Antimonium tartaricum.*
Thuja occidentalis (tree of life)	Purulent external otitis, chronic skin conditions such as warts, tumours.
Urtica urens (stinging nettle)	Burns, allergies, agalactia (lack of milk), urticaria.
Veratrum album (white hellebore)	Colicky diarrhoea, with weakness.
Zincum metallicum (zinc)	Nervousness, nervous tremor, weak bladder, paralysis of limbs and muscles.

Index